THE EARLY GUITAR

The famous Commedia dell'Arte actor, Carlo Cantù (1609-75) in the role of 'Mezzetino'.
Many guitar books include pieces with this title.
Engraving by Stephano della Bella. (*Courtesy Robert Spencer.*)

EARLY MUSIC SERIES: 4

THE EARLY GUITAR

A History and Handbook

by

JAMES TYLER

MUSIC DEPARTMENT

OXFORD UNIVERSITY PRESS

Ely House, 37 Dover Street, London W I X 4 A H

1980

ISBN 0 19 323182 4

Acknowledgments

We are grateful to the following for permission to reproduce illustrations:

The Trustees of the British Library: plates 1, 4b, 8, 10, 12, 13, 15, 20, 21, 22, 23, 24, 25, 27, 28, 29. Cambridge, Pepys Library, Magdalene College: plate 9; Editions Minkoff: plate 14; Henry E. Huntingdon Library and Art Gallery: plate 2; Iveagh Bequest, Kenwood: jacket illustration; Kunsthistorisches Museum, Vienna: plate 5; Musee Jacquemart-Andre, Paris: plates 3a-b; Robert Spencer: frontispiece and plate 6; Stadtbibliothek (Vadiana), St. Gallen: plate 4a; Gerry Young: plate 3c.

Printed in Great Britain by The Stellar Press Ltd, Hatfield, Herts
Bound by Henry Brooks Bookbinders Ltd

PREFACE

We are currently witnessing a widespread revival of music from the Middle Ages to the Baroque era. The publication of modern editions of early music and the extensive selection of recordings and live concerts of pre-1750 music can only be viewed as signs of an ever-increasing trend – a trend which is reaching audiences and performers from Japan and Australia to Europe and the Americas. The styles of playing, the sounds, and the brilliant tone colours of once-obsolete instruments are becoming familiar through the performances of a rich and excellent body of music, which is both new and fresh to our modern ears. The major renaissance plucked instrument, the lute, is once again regaining its former importance along with an array of other instruments in the lute family. And yet, the guitar remains all but left behind.

It is my sincere hope that this book will, at least, help to remedy this neglect. In the course of researching and writing it I have benefited greatly from the knowledge, practical experience, and co-operation of many people, especially David Fallows, Donald Gill, Colette Harris, Ian Harwood, Brian Jeffrey, Diana Poulton, John Roberts, Ephraim Segerman, Robert Spencer, and Anthony Mulgan and J. M. Thomson of the Oxford University Press. I owe a special debt of gratitude to Robert Spencer, who, so very generously, gave me much advice and information, allowed me to delve into his exceptional library of rare books and manuscripts, and gave much time and thought to reading and commenting on this book.

But, above all, it is my wife, Joyce, whom I owe for the actual appearance of the book at all! Her unwavering support and encouragement, her giving of countless hours to discuss ideas with me and to prevent me from too much woolly thinking, her polishing of my erratic prose style, and her labours in preparing the manuscript can never be adequately thanked.

CONTENTS

LIST OF PLATES

Frontispiece   Carlo Cantù (1609–75) in the role of 'Mezzetino'.

INTRODUCTION

It is the aim of this book to provide a useful and practical guide to the background, roles, and playing styles of the early guitar, and to present a survey of surviving guitar music from c.1546 to the end of the eighteenth century.

As there are no surviving instruments or music before approximately the end of the fifteenth century, it is both difficult and imprudent to write about the guitar before this period. The small number of pictures which survive from before the end of the fifteenth century allows us only to speculate about the instrument in the Middle Ages. I have therefore based the following definition on the instrument from the sixteenth century, when the exact nature of each of the different members of the guitar family became more clearly defined. The guitar is an instrument possessing, in most cases, a traditional 'figure-eight' or 'waisted' shape as seen from the front or back, and a flat or slightly rounded (vaulted) back when seen from the sides. It was designed, primarily, for use with gut strings. It has a neck which is distinctly longer than most contemporary plucked instruments, for example, the lute (i.e. one can usually place about eleven frets on the neck before reaching the body). All other features of the instrument, such as the style of the peghead, are mere details of personal taste and fashion and do not define the instrument.

Under this definition come the following instruments of the guitar family which will be discussed in this book. The *viola* or *vihuela* (*de mano*), a fairly large instrument, normally of six or more pairs of strings (courses), with a repertoire indistinguishable from that of the lute; the four-course guitar, a small instrument in the treble range with a repertoire quite distinctively its own; and the five-course guitar, a larger instrument than the four-course guitar, which became known as the 'Spanish guitar', and has the largest and most unique repertoire of the three. A range of other guitar variants will also be briefly noted.

In researching the early guitar, I have discovered that its repertoire before 1800 is huge, varied, fascinating, and second only to that of the lute. Surprisingly, the great majority of this abundant body of music is almost totally unknown to players today. The handful of pieces by a few well-known guitar composers, such as Robert de Visée and Gaspar Sanz is only the tip of the iceberg, and it was to make this fact commonly known that I was prompted to write this book.

Note: Abbreviated references to books and articles in the footnotes are expanded in the Bibliography.

PART ONE
HISTORY

I

ORIGINS: THE VIOLA OR VIHUELA

Writers, early and modern, unanimously agree that the guitar originated on the Iberian peninsula; yet the earliest visual and written references to the instrument come from early fifteenth-century Italian sources. Few, if any, records survive from the guitar's presumed place of origin, perhaps because this region, which was later to become Spain, was in a state of great economic decline during the period of the guitar's inception (except in the areas of Moorish civilization), with little cultural activity, an endless succession of plagues, and, consequently, a very small population.

The paintings of the Italians Sassetta and 'The Master of Vergil',[1] which date from the early fifteenth century, are the first to picture the 'figure-eight' shaped instrument with the flat back and rather long, fretted neck, which can safely be considered 'guitar-like'. With pre-fifteenth-century pictorial illustrations, it is really quite pointless to put the name 'guitar', to the countless instruments, bowed as well as plucked, which bear a vague resemblance in shape to the guitar as we know it. In some recent writings on the guitar, the entire subject of origins is thrown into confusion as a result of the fanciful excursions into antiquity by their authors, who point to various ancient Egyptian instruments as the direct ancestors of the guitar. This kind of uncritical and hasty guesswork, this labelling of a wide variety of available pictures with the name 'guitar', does nothing more than render the word meaningless.

A case in point is the fifteenth-century instrument illustrated in Plate 1, which has been labelled 'guitar' in most reference books because of the shape of its body, but which, in fact, is much more likely to be a *cetera* (cittern), because of the more important details of its fretting system and plectrum technique.[2]

We must also be careful not to assume that before the sixteenth century the terms *guitarra*, *chitarra*, *guiterne*, gittern, etc., meant what they came to mean in later centuries, i.e. guitar, because this was not always the case. Laurence Wright, in his brilliant and highly original article 'The Medieval Gittern and Citole: A Case of Mistaken Identity',[3] has shown that these terms (*guitarra*, *chitarra*, gittern, etc.), often meant not a guitar at all, but the tiny treble lute which, in the sixteenth century, became known as the

[1]Ravizza, E., pp. 81-2.
[2]Waldbauer, C., pp. 26-40.
[3]*Galpin Society Journal*, Vol. XXX (1977). I am indebted to Laurence Wright for letting me read his article prior to its publication. (See also Geiringer, Q.)

Plate 1

Cetera (cittern) from a set of Tarocchi cards. Italian, third quarter of the fifteenth century. Notice the fret system (shown as alterable wooden 'block' frets which can be re-arranged for different tones and semitones in contemporary *intarsia* pictures). The strings apparently go over the bridge to the bottom of the instrument, an arrangement typical of wire-strung instruments. The body shape is also found on some citterns of a later date. (See Buchner, M., Plate 186; or Praetorius, S., Plate VII.)

mandora. With these cautions very much in mind, we can proceed to an examination of the minute amount of information available to us from the fifteenth century.

While the kingdoms of the Iberian peninsula *per se* were, as previously mentioned, both economically and culturally bereft, the kingdoms of Naples and Sicily, then Spanish-speaking possessions of the House of Aragon, were thriving. As well as having strong political ties with the Papal Court in Rome, Naples was also closely associated with the small but wealthy and brilliant courts of Ferrara, Urbino, and Mantua, especially from the mid-fifteenth to the early sixteenth century. For example, Federigo da Montefeltro, whose court at Urbino was immortalized in Castiglione's *The Book of the Courtier* (1528), served the Aragonese dynasty of Naples in his capacity of military contractor. And the remarkable Isabella d'Este of Ferrara and Mantua (1474-1539) was the daughter of Eleanora of Aragon and the granddaughter of King Ferrante of Naples.

There is abundant evidence of musical activity in Ferrara beginning in the first quarter of the fifteenth century. Of particular interest are documents mentioning musicians such as Leonardo del Chitarino, employed at the court in 1424,[4] and Duke Leonello d'Este himself, who is known to have played the *chitarino* from at least 1437.[5] Also in Leonello's service at Ferrara was the most famous lute player of the century, Pietro Bono. Praised by princes and poets alike, he was known throughout his long career as Pietro Bono del Chitarino, though is often mentioned as playing the *liuto*, the *citara* (cittern), and the *violla* (*viola da mano*) as well.[6]

The term *chitarino* or *chitarrino* was used in the sixteenth century and later to mean the small four-course guitar, and, while it is tempting to assume that the fifteenth-century term meant the same instrument, this has yet to be proved. As previously stated, the term *chitarino*, *before* the sixteenth century, is just as likely to have meant a small treble lute.

The Italian term *viola* was used as a generic term for any stringed instrument, but it was also sometimes used more specifically to mean a guitar-like instrument, whether or not the qualifying words *da mano* were added; likewise, the Spanish term *vihuela de mano* or, simply, *vihuela*. To make a decision as to whether the term is being used generically or specifically, one must consider carefully the context of each individual reference. For example, when Castiglione in his *Book of the Courtier* speaks of singing to the *viola*, some modern translators automatically assume he meant the viol.[7] But, considering the long tradition of plucked instruments accompanying the solo voice, it is much more likely that he meant a *viola da mano*, or, perhaps, a lute (i.e. that he is

[4] Lockwood, P., p. 119.
[5] Ibid., p. 118.
[6] Ibid., p. 118, n. 11.
[7] Later in the book, after speaking of keyboard music, Castiglione also mentions *viole da arco*, which I take to mean viols. He therefore seems to be making a definite distinction between the plucked and bowed instruments in his own terminology.

using the term, specially, to mean a *plucked* instrument). Sir Charles Hoby, in his 1561 translation of the book, changes the word to lute,[8] logical for Hoby since the *viola da mano* was not so much in use in England. Significantly, he did not translate *viola* to mean a viol.

An interesting manuscript which survives from the end of the fifteenth century, contains, on one of its few pages, a chart showing the notes (in tablature) on the fingerboard of the *viola* with the names of the notes in letters beneath.[9] The chart is headed, 'La mano ala viola' (the fingerboard of the *viola*), and indicates that the tuning is the same as that of the typical six-course lute known from the early sixteenth century (i.e. a^l, e^l, b, g, d, A), but with the unusual addition of a low seventh course tuned to E. Following this, there is what appears to be a short 'prelude', and a setting of *Fortuna vincinecta* (*Fortuna per ta crudelte* by Johannes Vincinet) for *viola* (in tablature) and for a melody instrument (in staff notation). The nature of the *viola* tablature leaves no doubt that the instrument intended is a guitar-like (plucked) instrument. Also significant is the fact that the music is in the Neapolitan style of Italian tablature, thus strengthening the idea that Naples and her close allies, Ferrara, Urbino, and Mantua are the places to look for information on the early instrument.

The famous poet Giovanni Filoteo Achillini (1466-1538) was one of the renowned *improvisatori*, who improvised poetry to an instrumental accompaniment. An engraving of him, c.1510, by the artist Marcantonio Raimondi shows Achillini playing a *viola* (Plate 2). It is likely that this is the sort of instrument which Achillini's contemporary, Castiglione, had in mind when he used the term, and for which the Bologna tablature (described above) was intended (although the manuscript calls for an instrument of seven courses and Achillini's instrument appears to have only five). The instrument is about as large as a modern guitar. Achillini's right foot is resting on its case, and, judging by the shape of the case, the *viola* appears to have had a slightly rounded, or vaulted, back, a construction feature often found on guitars from the late sixteenth to the eighteenth century.

Other visual evidence of guitar-like instruments in the early sixteenth century is shown in the beautiful and remarkable wood inlays, known as *intarsie*, found in the study of Isabella d'Este, which still survive intact in her palace at Mantua. One of these *intarsie*[10] depicts a finely-detailed instrument beside which is a *lyra da braccia*. Judging by the surrounding objects, the instrument appears to be rather small, with ten frets (the standard number for the later sixteenth- and seventeenth-century guitars). It has

[8]Strunk, S., pp. 281-85.

[9]The MS. is in Bologna (University Library MS. 596 HH2⁴) mentioned in Plamenac, S., p. 6. It is bound with a printed copy of Pietro Borgi, *Chi de arte matematiche ha piacere* . . . (Venice, 1484). I am greatly indebted to David Fallows for bringing this MS. to my attention. For a description of this MS. see Fallows, T. For another *viola* publication in Neapolitan tablature, see n. 16.

[10]For a reproduction of this *intarsie* see Tyler, R. G.

Plate 2
Five-course *Viola da mano*, c.1510. Engraving by Marcantonio Raimondi.

a very shallow body with an unusual single corner on each side; the ribs are fashioned in the concave manner typical of the time and found on several other surviving stringed instruments from this period. It is difficult to see whether the instrument has four or five courses, as the peg arrangement is not clearly depicted and some of the strings are missing. This instrument can safely be called a small *viola*.

The composer-theorist Johannes Tinctoris wrote a few words about the *viola* in his book *De inventione et usa musicae*, written in about 1487 when he was employed at the court in Naples. Tinctoris first speaks of the lute and then of 'that, for example, invented by the Spanish, which both they and the Italians call the *viola*, but the French the *demi-luth* [dimidum leutum]. This *viola* differs from the lute in that the lute is much larger and tortoise-shaped, while the *viola* is flat, and in most cases curved inwards

19

on each side'.[11] Later, he speaks of 'the instrument invented by the Catalans, which some call the *ghiterra* and others the *ghiterna*. It is obviously derived from the lyre since it is tortoise-shaped (though much smaller) and has the same stringing and method of playing'. Here, with the term *ghiterra*, he seems to be describing the little treble lute later known as the *mandora*. Still later, he says: 'While some play every sort of composition most delightfully on the lute, in Italy and Spain the *viola* without the bow is used.'

Information about the *viola* (or *vihuela*) remains very sparse indeed until the early sixteenth century. A *vihuela de mano* from this period survives at the Musée Jacquemart-André of the Institut de France in Paris, and a description of it has been given by Michael Prynne.[12]

The instrument is quite large, having a body length of 58.4 cm., and, judging from signs of the original bridge position, a vibrating string length of about 80 cm. (Plates 3a, b, c). This would indicate that this *vihuela* is not the instrument which would have been used to play the later solo repertoire, but the bass of the *vihuela* family which was used to provide the simpler bass parts in a plucked ensemble.

The back of the instrument is flat and the construction of the back and sides is very unusual, being made up of alternate sections of dark and light woods fitted together like a jig-saw puzzle. The sound box is remarkably shallow, much more so than on a modern guitar, or, indeed, than on most of the modern attempts at reconstructing *vihuelas*. The belly is of pine and has not only the usual main sound hole but four auxiliary ones as well. These are decorated with rosettes made from layers of parchment. It originally carried twelve pegs for a string arrangement of six courses. The general appearance of this *vihuela* is in accordance with the few contemporary Spanish pictures of *vihuelas*.

In 1536 the first book of tablature for the *vihuela* was published, Luis Milán's *Libro de musica de vihuela de mano: Intitulado El Maestro . . .*[13]. The music requires a six-course instrument tuned, from the first course downward, to a fourth, a fourth, a major third, a fourth, a fourth. This is the same standard interval relationship as for the sixteenth-century lute. No specific pitch is indicated, nor would there have been, since at this time a standard and specific pitch was only a relative concept and each player tuned to whatever pitch suited his own strings, instrument, and personal inclination.[14]

Milán's music is well known today as a result of its use in the repertoire of the modern guitar. It includes a well-graded series of fantasias, intabulations of vocal pieces, songs for voice and *vihuela*, and six *pavanas* (courtly dances), some of which are

[11]Baines, F., pp. 22-4.
[12]Prynne, S., pp. 22-7. Robert Spencer informs me that the lutenist Oscar Ohlsen of Santiago, Chile, reports a *vihuela* preserved in a church in Quito, Ecuador.
[13]Fully described in Brown, I., pp. 47-50.
[14]Relative pitches are discussed in Ward, V., pp. 39-43 and in Ward, P.

Plates 3a, b
Vihuela, c.1500, Spain. Musée Jacquemart-André, Paris.

Plate 3c
Reconstruction of the same *vihuela* by Maish Weisman, London, 1976.   *Photo: Gerry Young*

21

based on Italian themes. The music, like contemporary lute music, is for the most part in a contrapuntal style, with sections of single-line running passages in some of the songs and fantasias. This strongly contrapuntal style is typical of the other six tablature collections for the *vihuela*, published in the sixteenth century.[15] Milán's book is an excellent tutor, and the music contained within it is of the highest quality. A recent edition with an English translation of the text makes available all of Milán's important detailed comments on almost every piece in the book; a perfect guide to the courtly art of *vihuela* playing.[16]

The year 1536 also saw the publication of an interesting collection of music for the *viola da mano* entitled *Intavolatura de viola overo lauto cioe recerate, canzone Francese, motette, composta per lo eccelente e unico musico Francesco Milane . . .*[17] It contains some of the finest music of the early sixteenth century by the most renowned lutenist of his day, Francesco da Milano. Published in Naples, it consists of two volumes, each containing pieces in both the normal Italian tablature and in the Neapolitan-style tablature. Written for either the six-course *viola* or the lute, these two volumes may be the earliest sources of Francesco's compositions.[18]

Juan Bermudo published his *Libro primo de la declaracion de instrumentos* in 1549 and expanded it in 1555. It is a book of music theory which deals with plainsong, polyphony, and the performance of music for keyboard and plucked instruments. Bermudo's

[15]These are listed in Brown, op. cit. as:

1538₁ Luis de Narváez: *Los seys libros del Delphin de musica . . .*

1546₁₄ Alonso Mudarra: *Tres libros de musica en cifras para vihuela . . .*

1547₅ Enriquez de Valderrábano: *Libro de musica de vihuela . . .*

1552₇ Diego Pisador: *Libro de musica de vihuela . . .*

1554₃ Miguel de Fuenllana: *Libro de musica para vihuela . . .*

1576₁ Esteban Daza: *Libro de musica en cifras para vihuela . . .*

In addition to these, there are also the following Spanish books, the music of which is described as being suitable for keyboard, harp, or *vihuela*:

1557₂ Luis Venegas de Henestrosa: *Libro de cifra nueva . . .*

1578₃ Antonio Cabezón: *Obras de musica . . .*

For valuable, detailed information concerning intabulation and theory for *vihuela*, see:

1555₁ Juan Bermudo: *Comiença el libro llamado declaracion de instrumentos musicales . . .*

In Brown, I., p. 89, is a description of some manuscript *vihuela* tablature found at the end of 1564₁₄. Another *vihuela* tablature is Madrid, Biblioteca Nacional, MS. 6001 (Ramillete de Flores MS. 1593) published in modern transcription and in tablature by Juan José Rey (Madrid, 1975).

[16]Jacobs, M.

[17]See the report of the recent discovery of these volumes in Giraud, R., pp. 217-19. There is a facsimile reprint of both volumes published by Minkoff (Geneva, 1977). See the section on Tablature in this book for a description of Italian tablature. The Neapolitan tablature used in the two volumes as well as in the earlier Bologna manuscript differs from it only in that '1' represents the open strings, '2' the first fret, etc., and the six lines represent the six courses with the highest line as the first course in Neapolitan tablature.

[18]For a modern edition of some of the music, see Ness, M. The tuning used in the '*Viola*' edition is, of course, the same as that for the lute of the period.

writings are a mine of information about, among other things, all the current procedures for playing the *vihuela*, guitar, and *bandurria*. Included also is information about the *discante* (sometimes called the *vihuela menor*), which is a small six-course treble instrument, tuned to the same interval pattern as other *vihuelas* and lutes, but up to a fifth higher in pitch than the standard *vihuela* (f.98).

Bermudo calls the courses for the standard *vihuela*: A, d, g, b, e¹, a¹ or G, c, f, a, d¹, g¹, which are also the tunings of the normal lute. But bear in mind that these are not necessarily to be equated with modern absolute pitch. He also says that for the purpose of intabulating vocal music, you can imagine [*imaginar*] the strings to be at any step of the scale you might prefer (f.29ᵛ).

There is evidence that the *vihuela* was strung in unison strings throughout, and not in octaves on the fourth, fifth, and sixth courses as on the lute. Diego Pisador, in his *vihuela* book of 1552, says that, as far as the fourth course is concerned, 'one of the fourth [strings] must be gently plucked and then matched with the other, which is not higher or lower' (f.A¹¹ᵛ). A later source, Covarrubias's *Tesoro* [Dictionary] of 1611, says that guitars have octave stringing, not unisons like *vihuelas* (p. 670 of the modern edition). Adrian Le Roy, in the 1574 English translation of his lute book, mentions (f.4) the Neapolitan player, Fabrice Dentice, as one who uses unisons, not octaves in the basses. On the other hand, it was probably as difficult to find good, plain gut strings of sufficient quality to be used as pairs of unisons in the bass of the *vihuela*, as it was to find them for the lute, and perhaps few players could afford the luxury. Wound strings did not come into use until the mid-seventeenth century.[19]

Bermudo also describes a seven-course *vihuela* with the following two tunings (again not to be taken as absolute pitches): G¹, D, G, d, g, d¹, g¹ (for which it would be most difficult to find strings), or G¹, D, G, B, f♯, b, d¹ (f.95ᵛ-6). Antonio Cabezón also describes a seven-course *vihuela* in his 1578 book (f.5). Eight-course *vihuelas* are mentioned in Francisco Pachero's 1599 manuscript, *Libro de descripcion de verdaderos*,[20] and in Scipione Cerreto's *Della prattica musica . . . 1601*, where it is referred to as a *viola Napolitano* (pp.155-9).

As can be gathered from visual evidence, descriptions, and the Paris instrument, *violas*, or *vihuelas* had the characteristic waisted shape to the sound box; an apparently shallow depth; at least five courses, usually six; came in many different sizes; had a bridge that was a narrow bar of wood glued to the table; used plain gut strings; had a fingerboard which was flush with the table, not raised as on the modern guitar; and, like the lute, used movable, gut frets tied around the neck. (Movable frets allowed for accurate tuning adjustments and compensations not available on a modern guitar. Vihuelists placed great importance on fine tuning; note Luis Milán's specific instruc-

[19] Abbott and Segerman, S.
[20] Ward, V., p. 11.

23

tions to move certain frets slightly for pieces in certain keys.)

As *vihuela*, *viola*, and lute music was identical in all outward respects (except perhaps in regional style), it is not surprising that *vihuela* music turns up later in the century as lute music in the important anthologies published by Pierre Phalèse, the Antwerp printer (who also anthologized four-course guitar music). Another witness to the practical interchangeability of these instruments was Bartholomeo Lieto Panhormitano, who published a treatise on the technique of intabulating, entitled *Dialogo Quarto de musica . . . per intavolare . . . con viola da mano over liuto . . .* (Naples, 1559). For him, there was no real difference between the two instruments, soundbox construction notwith-standing.

This belief in the interchangeability of the *viola*, *vihuela* and lute extends to modern times, exemplified by the modern edition of the manuscript known as 'The Bottegari Lutebook'[21] (Modena, MS. C311, bearing the date 1574). The editor apparently assumed that its ordinary Italian tablature is for the lute. Yet one of Bottegari's rubrics, in which he gives tuning instructions for a song accompaniment, reads: '. . . *bisogna accordare il canto della viola, cioè, il tenore*'. It seems clear from this statement that the instrument for which Bottegari wrote his fantasias and song accompaniments was not the lute, but the *viola*. Bearing in mind the late date, the fact that Bottegari was a Florentine with no apparent Neapolitan connections and, further, that he specifically uses the word *viola* rather than the more common word *liuto* (a word which he surely would have used had he meant it, and one which he never uses in the manuscript), it appears that this manuscript should perhaps be known as 'The Bottegari *Viola* Book'.

To summarize Chapter I, we have seen that the figure-eight shaped, plucked instruments under discussion cannot, with any certainty, be traced back earlier than the fifteenth century (given our present degree of knowledge); that the terms *guitarra*, *chitarra*, etc., though often found in literary sources from the Middle Ages, cannot positively be taken to mean the 'guitar' until the sixteenth century; that we do, how-ever, encounter the term *viola* or *vihuela* in the fifteenth century, and that these, aside from their use as generic terms to mean any stringed instrument, were often used specifically to mean a plucked instrument; that our earliest documentary information about the *viola* comes from Italian courts, such as those in Ferrara and in Spanish-influenced Naples; and that the Spanish called the instrument the *vihuela*, and from 1536 a fine repertoire of tablatures (in style and technical considerations virtually indistin-guishable from lute tablatures) was published for it.

It is not my intention here to delve too deeply into the repertoire of the *vihuela*, as the subject has often been dealt with elsewhere.[22] Instead, let us proceed to the species of *vihuela* known as the guitar.

[21]MacClintock, B.
[22]For example, Myers, V., Ward, V., Simpson and Mason, S., and Hall, P.

2

THE FOUR-COURSE GUITAR

The Spanish called it *guitarra*; the Italians, *chitarra da sette corde*, or *chitarrino*; the French, *guiterre*, or *guiterne*; and the English called it the gittern, from the French term.[1] The earliest music for it, which appeared in Alonso Mudarra's *vihuela* book of 1546, consists of one fantasia in 'temple viejos' (old tuning), and three more in 'temple nuevos' (new), a *pavana*, and a setting of 'O guardame las vacas', using the old Italian Romanesca ground. Although a modest offering, these are of the same exceptionally high quality as Mudarra's pieces for the six-course *vihuela*.

Mudarra describes the *guitarra* as having ten frets and a *bordón* on the fourth course. Its tunings and stringing were explained by Juan Bermudo in his 1555 book. Here he describes the guitar as being smaller than the *vihuela* (*mas corto*), and as usually having only four courses, the interval arrangement resembling the second to fifth courses of a *vihuela*. For specific tuning, he gives the following (Roman numerals designate the courses): (*Libro Quarto, Capitulo LXV*).

Ex. 1

The first three courses are in unison and the fourth has a *bordón* at the octave below.[2] The relative pitch is higher than the second to fifth courses of a *vihuela*, making the guitar a treble instrument. As we shall see later, the fourth course was sometimes a pair of unison strings, above the third course in pitch, which created a re-entrant tuning.

In Italy Melchior Barberiis's lute book *Opera Intitolata Contina . . . Libro Decimo* (1549) contains four fantasias for the guitar. Actually, they are light dance pieces, and one of

[1] The sixteenth-century gittern is not to be confused with the earlier instrument of the same name which, in fact, is a small treble lute. See Wright, G.

[2] The term *bordón* clearly means the thicker, gut, 'bass' string, which is tuned an octave below its thinner companion in the same course. The French used the term *bourdon*.

them was later reprinted in Paris as a *branle* (country dance). Barberiis called his instrument the *chitara da sette corde*, referring to the seven strings arranged in four courses, the first being single (as was sometimes found on the lute). Visual and written evidence confirms that this fashion for using only a single first string was quite widespread and also extended to the five-course guitar in the seventeenth and eighteenth centuries, even though virtually all the guitars which survive from this period were made to accommodate a double first course. This curious anomaly is nowhere explained, though we do know that it was very difficult to find treble strings of gut with equal thickness throughout their length, a requirement for good intonation. The problem of finding two matching strings was even greater, hence a single first course was probably a matter of simple practicality.

It was in France that the four-course guitar received the greatest attention. Starting in 1550, with the publications of Guillaume Morlaye, Simon Gorlier, Gregoire Brayssing (actually an expatriate German), and Adrian Le Roy, we are provided with a delightful repertoire of excellent fantasias for the solo guitar, dances in which the guitar can perform as the lead instrument in a consort, and chansons for voice with guitar accompaniment.

The guitar appears to have been favoured by the French King Henry II himself, who probably became acquainted with it during his four years as a Spanish hostage. But French court music was even more influenced by the Italians; Henry employed many Italian musicians, and, further, many of the guitar pieces in the first French books originated in Italy – the dances, for example, and the exquisite guitar fantasias written by Henry's court lutenist, Alberto da Rippa.[3]

Eventually, however, native French music came to predominate, with the publications of guitar intabulations of chansons by Sermisy, Certon, and others, and of numerous *branles*. This material later reached the rest of Europe with the help of the Flemish reprints of Phalèse, published in 1570 and 1573.

Accurate illustrations of the four-course guitar are found in these French publications (Plates 4a, b), which picture instruments having ten frets on the neck; a lute-type bridge (quite different from the modern guitar bridge with its raised 'saddle'), and a choice of a flat peghead with the pegs inserted from behind, or a pegbox with the pegs inserted from the side, as on viols or violins. The stringing, as deduced from the French tablatures, probably used a *bourdon* on the fourth course, as does the stringing for Spanish music. The French books also require two different tunings: the normal one, equivalent to Mudarra's 'temple nuevos', and 'a corde avalée' ('lowered') equivalent to the 'temple viejos'.

---

[3]The fantasias are published in modern edition with the tablature under Appendix ii of *Oeuvres d'Albert de Rippe I*, Centre National de la Recherche Scientifique, Paris (1972). However, many printing errors from the original tablature remain uncorrected in this edition.

LE
PREMIER LIVRE DE
CHANSONS, GAILLARDES, PAVANNES,
Branfles, Almandes, Fantaifies, reduictz en tabulature de Guiterne
par Maiftre Guillaume Morlaye ioueur de Lut.

A PARIS.
De l'Imprimerie de Robert GranIon & Michel Fezandat, au Mont
S. Hylaire, à l'Enfeigne des Grandz Ions.
I 5 5 2.
Auec priuilege du Roy.

Plate 4a
Typical four-course guitar illustrated on the title page of G. Morlaye, *Le Premier Livre* (1552).

Plate 4b
Four-course guitar illustrated in Mersenne, *Harmonie Universelle* (Paris, 1636), but copied from the Phalèse Guitar Book of 1570.

The French repertoire for this little guitar ranges from technically easy, but delightful, settings of popular music, to quite demanding intabulations of vocal music and fantasias. The fantasias of Morlaye, Brayssing, and da Rippa (in Morlaye's fourth book) are all of a high standard and deserve the attention of guitarists wishing to add to their concert repertoires. The dances and chansons in Le Roy's books are often set out twice, the first, a plain unembellished setting, the second, *plus diminuée*, with florid running passages similar to the virtuoso versions found in the lute books of the time. Admittedly, some of the pieces in these books are slight and unimaginative, but that is only to be expected in collections of this size, and, in any case, the excellent pieces more than make up for the lesser ones. In most of this repertoire the little guitar, tuned as Bermudo describes, carries the melody and does the florid passage work, playing as much of the bass as is possible on a treble instrument. For those wishing to enhance the bass line, there are innumerable other versions of the songs and dance pieces in many contemporary Parisian publications, and these can easily be used to form duet and ensemble versions with a proper bass and inner parts.[4] Playing plucked instruments in ensemble was clearly a quite common practice of the time. Bermudo describes the guitar, with *vihuelas*, etc., as making an excellent ensemble (f.98). A revival of this practice would certainly be in order.

In addition to playing in ensembles with other instruments, the little guitar was also used to accompany the voice. Fuenllana's *vihuela* book of 1554 contains a section of music, including a *villancico* by Juan Vasquez, 'Covarde cavallero', and a romance, 'Passeavase el Rey moro', in which the notes of the melody lines within the four-line Italian tablature itself are printed in red; the other accompanying notes are printed in ordinary black numbers. This style of notation is found only in Spanish sources, and the same arrangement applies in the *vihuela* books for the six-course instrument.[5] Fuenllana follows the vocal music with six fantasias for the guitar.

Adrian Le Roy's second and fifth books are entirely for solo voice and guitar, using a separate part in staff notation for the voice. As is the case in many lute and *vihuela* books (where staff notation is found), the player is told at the beginning of each piece to play a certain string and fret in order to give the singer his beginning pitch. The staff notation is sometimes, visually, in a different key from the instrumental accompaniment, but this is for the convenience of printing the entire melody line on the five-line stave, and to avoid having to use ledger lines which are difficult for a printer to set up. This fact has often been misunderstood or disregarded by editors of modern editions of lute and *vihuela* songs. By taking the key, or pitch, of the vocal line literally, they have led players to believe that they must use instruments of many outlandish pitches and sizes

---

[4] See Brown, I. for concordances.
[5] It should be noted that the recent facsimile editions of Luis Milán's and Diego Pisador's books from the firm of Minkoff have been printed entirely in black and white, thus rendering substantial portions of these books useless!

to accommodate the vocal line. When confronted with such questionable demands, always go back to the original source and follow the composer's directions.

During this same period, the guitar also became popular in England. The earliest mention of it seems to have been in Thomas Whythorne's famous autobiography, in which he says that in 1545 he 'learned to play on the Gittern, and Sittern which ii instruments were then strange in England, and therefore the more desyred and esteemed'.[6]

In 1568, James Rowbotham published *The breffe and playne instruction to lerne to play on the gyttron and also the cetterne*, in London.[7] Unfortunately, no copy of this book survives. In the same year, Rowbotham printed an English translation of one of Adrian Le Roy's lute books, calling it *A briefe and easye instruction to lerne to play on the lute*; this was the first lute tutor ever printed in England. The date, the publisher, and the wording of the title of the guitar and cittern book suggest that this too was a translation of one of Le Roy's books. If so, we have a reasonably good idea of the sort of guitar music which was played and heard in Elizabethan England.

A few English manuscripts of the period also contain examples of the English guitarist's repertoire. The earliest, Raphe Bowle's lute book, dated 1558 (London, British Library, Stowe 389), contains an untitled and incomplete setting for guitar of the Italian 'Passamezzo Antico' ground. Another lute manuscript (Osborne collection, Yale University Library), contains short versions of twenty-one popular pieces such as, 'When raging love', 'In winters just return' (both music to poems in *Tottel's Miscellany*), Italian grounds such as the *passamezzo antico* and *matazina*, and even the famous Spanish chord sequence, *Conde claros*. The remaining source, a keyboard manuscript compiled by Thomas Mulliner, contains some cittern and 'gitterne' tablature from about 1570. The two guitar pieces can be identified as the Italian grounds, *chi passa* and the *passamezzo antico*. All the guitar music in these manuscripts requires a four-course guitar and is notated, as was the fashion in England, in French tablature.

The Elizabethan guitarist, then, played the same range of material as his colleagues on the Continent, as well as native English popular music, and the guitar was probably a good deal more popular in England than these few musical remains suggest.[8]

The Flemish publisher, Pierre Phalèse, and his partner, Jean Bellère, published a sizeable anthology of guitar music in 1570. It contains one hundred and eighty-two pieces, reprinted, or, as some would say, pirated, from many of the previously printed books of Adrian Le Roy and others. As well as printing pieces identified from surviving sources, Phalèse does us the invaluable service of preserving many pieces from guitar books which have not survived. Also of interest are the instructions for the guitar with which he begins the book, although these turn out, in part, to be garbled instructions

[6]Osborne, W., pp. 19-20.
[7]Brown, I., p. 238.
[8]For further information on the guitar in England at this time, see Heartz, E.

for the cittern.[9] Like many of today's publishers of popular music, Phalèse appears to have been motivated by a desire to capitalize quickly on the popularity of the instrument, without making too great an effort at producing something new and original. The anthology must certainly have been well received by the public, for Phalèse is known to have published a reprint of it (or, perhaps, a different anthology), now lost, in 1573.

In Italy, Girolamo Giuliani published his *Intavolatura de Chitara* some time in the 1580s, yet another book which is now lost to us. We can only assume that it was for the four-course instrument.

Still surviving, though from the early seventeenth century, is a manuscript found in the Bibliothèque Royale du Conservatoire, Brussels (MS.24.135), which contains nineteen pieces in Italian tablature, almost all of them popular tunes of the day such as 'La Franceschina,' 'Ruggiero,' 'Spagnoletta,' and 'Matazina.' A similar manuscript is in the fine library of Robert Spencer in London.

Sometimes, when working with these Italian sources, it is difficult to decide whether or not the fourth course requires a *bourdon* string, as it does for the Spanish and most of the French tablatures. We know that, often, the Italians used a re-entrant tuning without a *bourdon*, as indicated by Scipione Cerreto in his *Della Prattica Musica* (1601). Cerreto gives unusually precise instructions for tuning the small four-course guitar. In staff notation and verbal description, he offers the following:

Ex. 2

The fourth course is in unison and the tuning is re-entrant, as for the cittern,[10] and similar to that described in certain five-course guitar sources, which will be discussed later. Despite this, Cerreto's tuning is like Bermudo's 'old tuning', but a tone higher. This tuning and its high pitch are corroborated in an anonymous collection, engraved in 1645, entitled *Conserto Vago* (Pleasant Consort), an excellent suite consisting of a 'Balletto', 'Volta', 'Corrente', 'Gagliarda', and a 'Canzone Franzese', all based on the same thematic material, and written for a trio consisting of *tiorba*, *liuto*, and *chitarino*.

---

[9]See Dobson, T. The instructions were first translated by Heartz (in Heartz, E.), on the assumption that they were a Latin translation of an Adrian Le Roy work. Heartz's interpretation of the tuning and stringing of the four-course guitar should be amended in the light of recent research. (See Tyler, R. G., p. 347, n.18.)

[10]Tyler, C. Notice also that this tuning is similar to that of certain small guitars in South America today (see Sensier, G., pp. 16-17), and is also one of the tunings of the modern ukulele.

The fact that the music requires the normal a[1] tuning of the lute and theorbo means that the little guitar is pitched just as Cerreto described. The guitar part, of course, is the treble of the ensemble and has the florid running figures which suit it so well. On the book's title page, the guitar is described as 'alla Napolitana', and, as Cerreto was also a Neapolitan and published in Naples, this tuning and stringing may form a distinct category in itself. The Neapolitan guitar was also to be found in the household of the composer, Carlo Gesualdo, Prince of Venosa. Apparently, he, his lute player Fabritio Filomarino, and Don Ettore Gesualdo 'played it excellently in concert'. [11]

Earlier, in the sixteenth century, some *chitarini . . . alla Napolettana* are known to have been used in the lavish music written for the wedding celebrations in 1589 of Ferdinand I de' Medici in Florence. A *chitarella Spagnola* was used as well. [12] Emilio de' Cavalieri also employed a *chitarina alla Spagnuola* in ensemble with other instruments in his important dramatic oratorio, *Rappresentazione di Anima et di Corpo* (1600).

A further reference to the guitar's use in full ensemble was made by Agostino Agazzari in 1601. He wrote: '[like ornament instruments] are those which, in a playful and contrapuntal fashion, make the harmony more agreeable and sonorous, namely, the lute, *theorbo*, harp, *lirone*, cittern, spinet, *chitarrino*, violin, pandora [i.e. *mandora*] and the like'.

A beautiful *chitarrino* from this period survives in the instrument collection in Vienna. [13] Made by Giovanni Smit in Milan (1646), it has a vaulted back made of separate strips of dark wood with ivory fillets in between. The sounding string length is approximately 51cm. It is precisely the sort of instrument on which to play the 'playful and contrapuntal' running figures found, for example, in the *Conserto Vago* (Plate 5).

Most of the music mentioned heretofore was written in the lute style, called 'punteado' by the Spanish and 'pizzicato' by the Italians, in which single notes are plucked separately. But the guitar was also strummed, and the music notated in a shorthand system that indicated only which full chords should be sounded. This style of playing will be discussed fully in the next chapter dealing with the five-course guitar, but it should be noted here that the four-course guitar also made full use of the strummed style of playing. For example, Pietro Millioni in his 1627 book includes a chord chart for both types of instrument, and the music he provides is entirely to be strummed. He calls the larger instrument by its usual name, *chitarra spagnola*, and the four-course instrument, the *chitarrino overo ghitarre italiana* (little guitar, or Italian guitar). There were an enormous number of books published which contained music using only the strumming style, and, although usually intended for the larger instrument, the small guitar could also be used, thus increasing its repertoire considerably.

[11]See C. MacClintock, trans.: Vicenzo Giustiniani, *Discorso sopra la Musica* (*c.1628*) (Rome, 1962), p. 79.
[12]Brown, S., pp. 131-2.
[13]Baines, E., p. 47.

Plate 5
Chitarrino by Giovanni Smit, 1646. Vienna Kunsthistorisches Museum, C.53.

Although the weight of evidence indicates that the four-course guitar was normally a small one, there is one source which gives, not only the tuning appropriate for a small instrument, but another which suggests a larger one. Michael Praetorius in his *Syntagma Musicum*, ii (1619), gives us the following two tunings without mentioning details of stringing:

Ex. 3

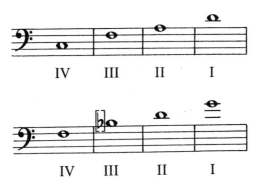

His first tuning of a fourth lower than the second, must, if we accept this as an absolute pitch, be for a larger instrument.

Elsewhere in his book Praetorius says, 'The *Quinterna* or *Chiterna* [his terms for the guitar] is an instrument with four courses which are tuned like the very earliest lutes' (p.53). He mentions that the *quinterna* has double strings (p.49), and that 'it has however not a rounded back, but is completely flat, quite like a bandora, and hardly two or three fingers in depth. . . . Some have five courses, and, in Italy, the charlatans and mountebanks [Ziarlatini und Salt'in banco], who are like our comedians and clowns, strum them, singing their *villanellas* and other foolish songs. Nevertheless, good singers can sing fine and lovely songs with it' (p.53).

From his tuning chart we can see that Praetorius is thinking of a guitar with a *bourdon* on the fourth course and not the re-entrant tuning of Cerreto in Naples.

The last known publication written specifically for the small four-course guitar comes to us from England near the time of the Restoration. John Playford provides us with *A Booke of New Lessons for the Cittern and Gittern* (1652). One of this well-known and important printer's earliest publications, it is a treasure trove of English ballad tunes and popular music, and is deserving of our attention and appreciation. In two sections, one for each instrument, it has a separate title page for each. Unfortunately, the same illustration of a man playing a cittern is printed on both title pages, so we are deprived of a view of the guitar Playford had in mind to play these tunes.

The guitar section, written in French tablature, offers forty-one extremely simple settings of pieces such as 'When the King enjoyes his own again', 'Canaries', 'Dr. Colman's Simphoney', 'Mr. Lawes Tune', 'Stingo, or Oyle of Barley', 'Gather your Rosebuds', 'Cuckold all a Row', 'Italian Rant', and 'Dull Sir John'. As solos entirely on their own (as printed) these tend to be rather shallow and unconvincing. But I suggest that when used to lead a consort, they can be extremely effective and quite charming.[14]

It is significant that the four-course guitar remained popular enough in England at this late date for Playford to go to the considerable bother and expense of printing tablature for it. It is also curious that Playford, astute businessman that he was,[15] did not foresee in 1652 that the five-course 'Spanish' guitar, which was already 'all the rage' on the Continent, would soon eclipse the four-course guitar and enjoy the same unprecedented popularity in Britain as well.

[14]Most of the pieces can be supplied with bass lines and ideas for variations. For concordances, see Simpson, B.
[15]Krummel, E., pp. 115-126.

3

THE FIVE-COURSE GUITAR

Visual evidence confirms that five-course, guitar-like instruments were in use from at least the end of the fifteenth century. (See the engraving by Raimondi, Plate 2.) At this time, the terms *viola* or *vihuela* were applied to these instruments, as well as to those with six or more courses. Certainly in the earliest source of music for the five-course instrument, Miguel Fuenllana's *Orphenica Lyra* of 1554, it was called the *vihuela de cinco ordenes* (*vihuela* of five courses), in order to distinguish it from the usual six-course instrument for which most of the music in this collection was written.[1] The five-course tablature calls for an instrument with a bottom fifth course tuned a fourth below the fourth course. No indication is given as to pitch or octave stringing. The instrument for which this five-course music was written could very well have been a large one, as distinct from the four-course *guitarra*, music for which, under this name, is also included in the book. Fuenllana's five-course music consists of two sections of a Mass by Morales, a *villancico* by Vasquez, and six excellent fantasias.

Juan Bermudo frequently referred to the *guitarra de cinco ordenes* in his *Libro primo de la declaracion de instrumentos* (1555), saying that one could be made by adding to the four-course guitar a string a fourth *above* the present first course (f.xxviii[v]). He also describes new and improved tunings such as: c, g, c[l], e[l], g[l] (f.xcvii–xcvii[v]). This pitch I assume from context. He further mentions a 'guitarra grande' of six courses (f.xciii), and gives more, rather unusual, tunings for the four-course guitar. No music survives for any of these tuning arrangements.

We are most fortunate to be able to relate Bermudo's small five-course guitar to an instrument, probably Portuguese, which survives from very nearly the same time. It is the superbly constructed guitar by Belchior Diaz, dated 1581, which is now in the Royal College of Music's collection in London.[2] It has a vaulted back constructed of seven quite deeply carved fluted ribs of the same dark, dense wood as the sides. These sides, even at the deepest part of the vaulted back, are quite shallow, conforming to Praetorius's description of 'two or three fingers high'. The instrument is intended for five double courses, and, with a string length of only 55cm., it could easily be tuned,

---

[1]Fuenllana, of course, also speaks of the *Vihuela de Quatro Ordenes, Que Dizen Guitarra* (the vihuela of four courses which is called guitar) f.IV.
[2]Described in Baines, E., p. 47.

even in modern, absolute pitch, to the c, g, c¹, e¹, g¹ mentioned by Bermudo, or, in a more usual interval arrangement, with the top course roughly at g¹. This type of small guitar would later be known in Italy as the *chitarriglia* (as distinct from the four-course *chitarrino*).

The rosette is missing from the Diaz guitar, but it probably resembled the one found, still intact, in the larger, 'Spanish' guitar, which is in the collection of Robert Spencer in London. Unlabelled, and with no identifying marks or stamps, it nevertheless has inlaid fingerboard decorations identical to those on the Diaz guitar. Its general appearance, workmanship, and style of construction place this guitar in the period somewhere between the late sixteenth century up to about 1600 (Plate 6). It is the only other guitar, besides the Diaz, which, to my knowledge, survives from the sixteenth century. Like the Diaz, it is somewhat heavier and more robust than examples from the later baroque era tended to be, and the workmanship is excellent. The rosette is made of carefully cut and built-up parchment. It has a flat back and is made for five pairs of strings. At one stage in its life the neck had been cut down to shorten the string length; many extant guitars now found in museums have been similarly tampered with at some stage. The instrument has recently been restored to its original state, as far as could be determined, and now has a string length of 68cm.

How was the standard-sized Spanish guitar tuned? We have seen that Fuenllana's music from 1554 requires the same basic intervals as the first five strings of the modern guitar, but we do not know at what specific pitch they were tuned. This interval arrangement, with *bourdons* on the fourth *and* fifth courses, was, as we shall see, a common one in Spain, and was used frequently for popular and strummed music.

Our next information comes from France and takes the form of a drawing by Jacques Cellier (c.1585), which includes the following tuning:[3]

Ex. 4

V   IV   III   II   I

[3]From Paris, Bibliothèque Nationale, MS. Fr. 9152. Reproduced in Turnbull, G., Plate 19. The drawing shows a four-course (seven-string) instrument with a tuning chart underneath for a five-course instrument. See also the copy of this MS. now in the British Library, described in Jeans and Oldham, D., pp. 30-1. The verbal instructions under the drawing are: 'La grosse corde de la guiterne saccorde avec la suivante a la quarte Et la suivante avec la quarte a la quarte'. This describes a four-course guitar as the drawing illustrates, but the staff notation tuning chart gives not only a tuning for a five-course instrument, but one in which the interval of the third course does not fit into the normal arrangement of guitar intervals known either before or after the date of the drawing. The instructions above leave us in confusion regarding the staff notes, and they can be interpreted in more than one way.

Plate 6
Guitar c.1600, in the collection of Robert Spencer.

37

As we have seen, a re-entrant tuning is known to have been used for the four-course guitar from Cerreto's 1601 book and was probably in use much before that date. (It was known to have been used for the cittern from at least the fifteenth century.)[4] I assume the single notes to represent the normal double courses tuned in unison, and the octave 'c's are included in order to make it clear that the fourth course was the only one to be octave strung. The third course interval conforms to none found in any tablatures for the guitar, nor to the other tunings encountered using d^1 as the pitch of the first course (e.g. Sanseverino, 1620, f.3^v). I suggest that this is a mistake and that the tuning in full should read:

Ex. 5

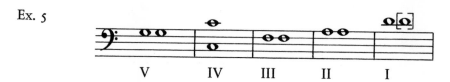

It will be noted that this re-entrant interval arrangement, although usually at the pitch e^1, is the major one used by the most important guitar composers of the baroque era.

The five-course Spanish guitar began its astonishing rise in popularity towards the end of the sixteenth century, and soon eclipsed the *vihuela*, *viola*, four-course guitar, and even, to some extent, the lute. The earliest source of music for it, if we exclude Fuenllana's *vihuela de cinco ordenes* material, is a manuscript from about 1595. This ushers in a whole new concept, unique to the guitar, of notating music and recording a style of playing which, before this date, had never been written down.

The manuscript, written in Italian by a Spaniard, Francisco Palumbi,[5] contains a system of notating strummed chords. The idea behind this notation was to assign a separate letter of the alphabet (or symbol) to each chord found on the fingerboard. The chords employ all five courses. Under the letters, a series of vertical lines are placed, either below or above one horizontal line to indicate, respectively, a down or an up stroke of the right hand. In Palumbi's and a few other systems, the alphabet letter itself is placed above or below. In later systems, more exact rhythm and metre are sometimes supplied by placing ordinary notes above the letters as in other tablatures. (A full explanation of the system, with its variants, is found in Part 2.) The Italian term *alfabeto* was used to designate this system, which was almost universally used in the following century. Although the letters used do not correspond to the actual names of the chords as we now know them, this system clearly foreshadows the chord symbol

[4]Tyler, C., pp. 25-9.
[5]Paris, Bibliothèque Nationale, MS. 390. 'Libro di Villanella Spagnuol 'et Italiane et sonate spagnuole . . .' Another, later, MS. by him is in Madrid, Biblioteca Nacional, MS. 14039, and also contains songs with *alfabeto* accompaniment (See Devoto, Q., pp. 3-16 and Danner, F., pp. 6-7.)

system which guitarists use in popular music today.

The music in the Palumbi manuscript consists of Italian and Spanish songs with their chordal accompaniments, as well as the chord sequences which are the bases of well-known dances, such as the *folia, ciaccona,* and *zarabanda.*

In 1596, Doctor Juan Carlos Amat[6] published his *Guitarra Española* in Barcelona.[7] In it, his chord system proves to be similar to Palumbi's, except that Amat assigns numbers instead of letters to each chord. He also gives more precise tuning instructions, this time at the nominal pitch which was soon to become standard. His verbal tuning directions give us the following:

 Ex. 6

Notice that *bourdons* are used on the fourth *and* fifth courses, and that the basic pitches are like those of the first five strings of the modern guitar.

Amat's book went through many editions, and remained in print until the early nineteenth century. It is interesting to note that, in all the editions, Amat advises that his chord system could also be used for the four-course guitar, a fact which suggests that the smaller instrument might have had a much longer life than previously thought. Later printers added more and more details to Amat's original material, such as including the *bandurria* and the *tiple* [treble guitar], instruments which were not included in the two editions which Amat himself edited.

---

[6]Juan Carlos is the spelling of the name on the title-page of the earliest surviving edition of his book (1626). This is the Castilian spelling as opposed to the Catalan, Joan Carles. Carles is apparently his father's surname, thus his principal surname, and Amat, found in later books, his mother's surname. Amat is the name he is known by today, and I retain it for the sake of uniformity. I am indebted to Jack Sage and Monica Hall for this information. Miss Hall has published an article on Amat's book, see Hall, G.

[7]No copies of this original edition exist, but there are later editions, including two which were published during Amat's lifetime (1572-1642). The first of these was printed in Lérida in 1626 (sole copy in Chicago, Newberry Library), and a reprint of it in 1627. There was a second edition published in Gerona in 1639. I am indebted to Brian Jeffery for bringing the 1626 copy to my attention. The bibliographical dates for Amat's book are most confusing, as the 1639 edition includes a reprinted letter in the preface, which says that 1586 is the date of the original. This is assumed to be a mistake, as Amat would have only been fourteen years old at this time! On the other hand, it is possible that Amat began to study the guitar when he was very young and did actually devise this quite simple chord notation in 1586. We have no precise idea of what the original little booklet contained, and the more sophisticated, theoretical material and a reworking and polishing of the chord system could possibly have been Amat's mature, seventeenth-century work. After all, the degree of musical complexity of Amat's chord system hardly approaches, say, that of Mozart's work when he was fourteen. If 1586 is the correct date, then Amat takes precedence over Palumbi in being the first to write down a chord notation. Of course, either system could be older still, but we lack the surviving sources to prove it.

Despite the long popularity of Amat's book, hardly any music which uses his system survives, except for a few minor examples in some other Spanish sources. Music using the Italian *alfabeto* system, on the other hand, is found in innumerable books and manuscripts, even in Spain, by such composers as Gaspar Sanz.

In 1606, with the publication of Girolamo Montesardo's book of *alfabeto* music for the five-course guitar, the Italians took the Spanish guitar and made it their own. Also bearing in mind that Italian music and musical style was a dominant force throughout Europe and England during the late sixteenth century and throughout most of the seventeenth, it should come as no surprise that the history of the guitar in the baroque era is primarily a history of Italian guitarists and the guitarists of other nationalities whom they influenced.

From 1606 to about 1629 the only known style of guitar music published (and found in manuscript) was that using the *alfabeto* system. The approximately sixty-nine books printed between these two dates contain hundreds of examples of Italian and Spanish dances, popular pieces, and songs with accompaniment. This repertoire, in the main, has not yet been performed in modern times. The music appears to be quite simple, even naive, until one realizes that what is printed is often only the bare 'skeleton' of the music and the performer is expected to use the exciting rhythmic embellishments and variations, intricate strumming patterns, and ornamentation which exist today only, perhaps, in Flamenco guitar music and, certainly, in the guitar music of Latin America. A selection of recordings of Paraguayan, Argentinian, or Mexican guitarists (who often use instruments not too far removed from those used by their baroque counterparts), can suggest to us one way of thinking about the performance of this deceptively simple *alfabeto* repertoire, for on these recordings can actually be heard performed the *picos*, *repiccos*, and other *batterie* (rhythmic strumming patterns) advocated by the writers of the late sixteenth- and seventeenth-century *alfabeto* books.

In France, music for the five-course guitar appears first in the publication *Metodo mui facilissimo para aprender tañer la guitarra a lo Español* by the Spanish composer Luis de Briçeño. Beautifully printed by Pierre Ballard, the book is dedicated to Madame de Cales.[8] It is written in Spanish chord tablature similar to Amat's, but using a different numbering of the chords, a system later to be known as 'Castilian', Amat's being 'Catalan'. As in other *alfabeto* books, the music consists of accompanied songs and the chords for dances, all of which are Spanish, or Spanish in form. The songs are difficult to reconstruct owing to our present scant knowledge of the melodies which should be employed, but the dances, simple and direct, present no problems. Briçeño explains carefully how the strings are to be tuned, and, assuming the pitch e¹ for the first course, the result is:

[8]For a translation of the preface see Roberts, G., p. 2.

Ex. 7

V   IV   III   II   I

I have previously mentioned a re-entrant tuning found earlier in France (J. Cellier, c.1585), but here we find one which uses no *bourdons* whatever. Strange as this arrangement may seem to the modern guitarist, it was often used by some of the most important early guitarists, including Gaspar Sanz.[9] The reason for this and other re-entrant tunings becomes clear when one works from the original tablatures, for the high fifth and, sometimes, fourth courses were used by guitarists to achieve a special effect, called by Sanz *campanellas* (little bells).[10] By employing as many open strings as possible, the notes of the scale passages are allowed to ring on, one note melting into the next in the manner of a harp or bells.

Tuned re-entrantly, the guitar is an alto or tenor range instrument, which, unlike the modern guitar or the lute, has no bass notes to speak of. For this reason, most early guitarists must have regarded the guitar as an instrument set quite apart from the lute, with its own unique styles of playing and its own distinct idioms. This may help to explain why the guitar retained only five courses for over two hundred and fifty years, while the lute during this period was constantly having additions made to its bass range.

Etienne Moulinié's *Airs de cour avec la tablature de luth et de guitarre . . .*, which was published in 1629, contains some French, Italian, and Spanish songs with the guitar chords fully written out in French tablature and the vocal part in staff notation.[11] The keys of the songs in the staff notation seem to indicate that a guitar with its top string tuned to d[1] was required, but this pitch, as we have seen, could be varied.

The theorist Marin Mersenne, in his *Harmonie Universelle* (1636), devotes a section to the guitar in which, after discussing both the four- and five-course instruments, he prints two short pieces in French tablature by a M. Martin.[12] Mersenne's tuning is the same as Briçeño's, but a tone lower than I have given, in d[1] (Plate 7).[13]

[9]See Murphy, T., p. 51.
[10]This is an aspect of early guitar music which modern editors often omit entirely from their publications, but which can be readily seen, understood, and played by the guitarist who can read tablature.
[11]I am indebted to Robert Spencer for bringing this source to my attention.
[12]Probably François Martin, whose guitar book of 1663 was recently discovered by David B. Lyons. Mr Lyons is planning to publish information on Martin and I am indebted to him for telling me about this source.
[13]See Chapman, M., pp. 134-140. It should be noted, however, that there is at least one French reference of the time (in Pierre Trichet's treatise, c.1640) to the use of *bourdons* on the fourth and fifth courses. (See Lesure, T., p. 156.)

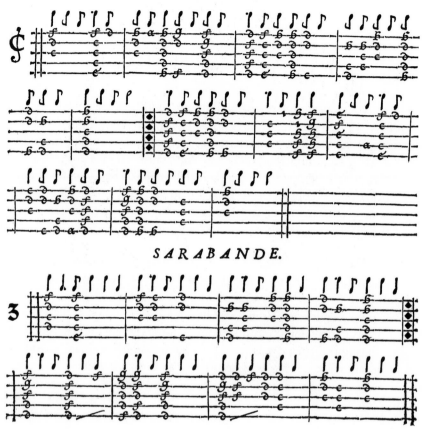

Plate 7

Allemande and Sarabande by 'Monsieur Martin' from Mersenne, *Harmonie Universelle . . . traité des instruments* (1636), p.97.

THE 'ITALIAN SCHOOL'

The first important guitar composer of the seventeenth century worked as a guitarist, lutenist, and theorbist in his native Italy, as well as in Brussels under the patronage of Archduke Albert, the Hapsburg ruler of the Spanish Netherlands. He was Giovanni Paolo Foscarini (Plate 8). We know few details of his personal life, but we do know that the much respected Albert purposefully gathered around him and supported some of the most brilliant artists and musicians of the day, the most outstanding being the painter, Rubens.

Plate 8
Giovanni Paolo Foscarini. Portrait from his *I quatro libri della chitarra spagnola* (c.1632).

Court life in Brussels must have been wonderfully stimulating for the young Foscarini, but it seems likely that when Albert died in 1621, Foscarini's circumstances changed quite dramatically as well, for we next hear of him in 1629, back in Italy (Ancona), when his *Intavolatura di chitarra spagnola, libro secondo* was published in the nearby town of Macerata. It must have been during this time that Foscarini became a member of the 'Academia dei Caliginosi', which was founded in Ancona in 1624. His academic name, 'Il Furioso' (the passionate one), was the name he used on the title pages of most of his books.

Libro primo is lost to us, and the *libro secondo* mentioned above contains only *alfabeto* style music, not too different from that which appeared in many other guitar books of the time. But around 1630 Foscarini published his *Primo, secondo, e terzo libro*, a book which marks a new departure, not only in Foscarini's music, but in guitar music in general. In it are found not only *alfabeto* pieces, but pieces which employ a mixture of that style with the *pizzicato* style notated in five-line Italian tablature. Foscarini's music is infinitely more sophisticated than that published by his contemporaries, and even by the standards of guitarists working later on in the century, he stands out as a very individual and quite exceptional composer for the guitar. Often daring and original, he clearly influenced many later players. Gaspar Sanz cites Foscarini among the 'masters of Rome'.

In addition to Rome, where he expanded his c.1630 work to five parts and published it, Foscarini appears to have also spent some time in Paris, where he published an Italian translation of Kepler's *Harmonices mundi* in 1647.[14] A letter survives, written by Foscarini in 1648 to the influential poet and friend of musicians, Constantin Huygens, which was sent from Paris.[15]

His last book is a 1649 Venetian reprint of his 1640 edition. Although he is mentioned in other guitarists's books after this date, we must assume that he died around this time. His music, which includes *toccatas, ciaccone, passacalli, folie, volte, gagliarde, alemande, sinfonie* with continuo, and some duets, deserves all the effort it would take to produce a satisfactory modern edition. His music belongs in the modern guitarist's repertoire.

During this same period, the name of the most renowned guitarist of the age is first mentioned. Francesco Corbetta (c.1615-1681), a native of Pavia, Italy, began his career as a teacher in the university town of Bologna, where he published his first modest collection of guitar pieces in 1639. The dedications in this book reveal that he taught and was patronized by many important noblemen and church dignitaries. While still in Bologna, he also taught a young student named Giovanni Battista Granata, who was later to become his chief rival.[16]

Corbetta's abilities soon earned him a post in the court of Carlo II, Duke of Mantua, to whom he dedicated his second book of guitar music, published in 1643. He then moved to Brussels, where he played at the court of Archduke Leopold Wilhelm, and then, in 1656, on to Paris, where he appeared in a court ballet under the direction of his expatriate countryman, Jean-Baptiste Lully, in which King Louis XIV himself performed one of the dancing roles. Some time in the 1660s he arrived in England where he was soon found in the company of King Charles II, who, while in exile on the Continent, knew Corbetta and was already an enthusiastic guitar player himself. It was not long before Corbetta was a firmly established figure in the musical life of the English court, and, as a result, the guitar very rapidly caught up with and surpassed in popularity even the lute, much to the annoyance of those who considered the guitar

---

[14]See Danner, F., p. 18.

[15]See Marcuse, S., p. 421.

[16]At one point, Corbetta actually accused Granata of plagiarism, an accusation not without grounds. The instructions for Granata's own 1646 book show him to have been a word-for-word plagiarizer of Foscarini as well!

an insignificant and unworthy upstart. One such person was the diarist Samuel Pepys, who believed himself to be quite an accomplished lute player, and noted in his famous diary this mixed reaction:

August 5, 1667

After done with the Duke of York, and coming out through his dressing room, I there spied Signor Francisco tuning his guitar, and Monsieur de Puy, with him who did make him play to me which he did most admirably – so well that I was mightily troubled that all that pains should have been taken upon so bad an instrument.

The inclusion in Pepys's library, which survives intact in Cambridge, of a guitar tutor by Cesare Morelli,[17] suggests that he too eventually succumbed to the lure of 'so bad an instrument' (Plate 9).

Plate 9
Samuel Pepys' own setting for voice, guitar, and continuo of Davenant's 'Beauty retire' (Cambridge, Pepys Library, Magdalene College, MS.2591, pp.210-211.)

[17]Cambridge, Pepys Library, Magdalene College, MS. 2805, dated 1680. His library also includes four extensive manuscripts of songs with guitar accompaniment, which include some of his own compositions! (MSS. 2591, 2802, 2803, 2804.)

Corbetta's music is some of the best written and confirms without question that his reputation was truly justified.[18] His suites, usually arranged by key, *toccatas*, and other individual pieces, especially from his 1643, 1648, and 1671 books, make substantial additions to the guitarist's repertoire; it is surprising that no satisfactory modern editions of these books have as yet appeared.

His most famous work is *La Guitarre Royalle dediée au Roy de la Grand Bretagne* (1671),[19] which, although printed in Paris, contains music, for the most part, connected with the court of its dedicatee, Charles II. Another work, *La Guitarre Royale* (1674), is dedicated to Louis XIV and contains music of a less demanding nature. Fortunately for the serious guitarist, facsimile editions of these two original tablatures are now available[20] (See Appendix 4).

Corbetta used the following tuning in most of his works:

Ex. 8

      V   IV   III   II   I

From about 1630, the number of publications for the guitar by Italian composers increased steadily. Works by the following composers were available from this time:

    G. P. Foscarini – 1629, c.1630, c.1632, 1640 (two editions), 1649

    P. Millioni – 1631, 1635, 1661, 1676

    G. B. Abbatessa – 1635, 1637, c.1650, 1652

    L. Monte – c.1636

    G. A. Colonna – 1637

    P. Millioni and L. Monte – 1637, 1644, 1647, 1652, 1659, 1666, 1673, 1678, 1684, 1737

    G. B. Sfondrino – 1637

    F. Corbetta – 1639, 1643, 1648, 1671, 1674

    A. Trombetti – 1639

    A. M. Bartolotti – 1640, c.1645, c.1655

[18]For details of Corbetta's life and work see Keith, G., pp. 73-93, and for a great deal of new biographical information see Pinnell, R.

[19]Allen, G. is an excellent and complete transcription which represents the music faithfully and includes the tablature, essential for serious study and performance.

[20]However, the Forni facsimile of the 1674 book does not contain the duet parts for the first twelve pieces. These are missing from the Bologna copy, but do survive in the Paris (Bibliothèque Nationale) copy.

A. Carbonchi – 1640, 1643

C. Calvi – 1646

G. B. Granata – 1646, c.1650, 1651, 1659, 1674, 1680, 1684

F. Valdambrini – c.1647, 1648

T. Marchetti – 1648, 1660, c.1665

S. Pesori – 1648, 1648, c.1650, c.1650, c.1650

D. Pellegrini – 1650

G. Banfi – 1653

G. Bottazzari – 1663

F. Coriandoli – 1670

F. Asioli – 1674, 1676

G. P. Ricci – 1677

N. Matteis – c.1680, 1682

L. Roncalli – 1692

A. Michele – 1698

I have limited the items listed above to books containing primarily solo music. To have added all the song books with guitar accompaniments published between 1606 and 1700 would have increased this list by pages. A number of the above items are reprints (such as Millioni's and Monte's *alfabeto* collection, which was first published in c.1627 and was still being reprinted as late as 1737), which only serves to reinforce that which the list already quite clearly indicates, that there was a palpable demand for guitar music in seventeenth-century Italy.

In the second half of the century, Italy was the scene of the greatest flowering of art music for the guitar in the history of the instrument. Without doubt, the works of Angiolo Michele Bartolotti, the prolific Giovanni Battista Granata,[21] Giulio Banfi, Francesco Coriandoli, Francesco Asioli, and Count Ludovico Roncalli, offer some of the most rewarding additions to the guitarist's repertoire. Roncalli is already somewhat familiar to us through the selections of his pieces which have appeared in modern editions; however, since these do not take into account the tuning which Roncalli used (i.e. that of Briçeño), his music is presented in a distorted fashion, as guitarists who have played these pieces from the original tablatures on a properly tuned instrument will be quick to confirm.

[21]His 1674 book, which includes a fine set of pieces for guitar, violin, and viola da gamba, as well as guitar solos, is available in a facsimile edition. (See Appendix 4.) His 1684 book also contains similar compositions, but the part books for violin and viola da gamba are now, unfortunately, lost.

Though the guitarists listed above have produced works of great merit, frustratingly little is known of their backgrounds, or professional lives. For example, Domenico Pellegrini's book of 1650 supplies us with the only shred of information we know about him. From its dedication and prefatory material, we can deduce that he was associated with the famous 'Accademia dei Filomusi' in Bologna, and would therefore have been a colleague of such eminent composers as Adriano Banchieri, Claudio Monteverdi, and, later, Giovanni Battista Vitali. And that, I'm afraid, is the full extent of our knowledge of Pellegrini to date. We can only hope that continued research will bring to light new information about all of these outstanding guitarist-composers.

THE 'FRENCH SCHOOL'

We have seen that the four-course guitar was very much appreciated in France in the sixteenth century, and that the Spaniard, Luis de Briçeño, created an interest in the five-course guitar in the second quarter of the seventeenth century. Surviving in Paris from this latter period are three very interesting manuscripts; one, dated 1649, contains solos, songs, and pieces for guitar and one and two viols (Bibliothèque Sainte Geneviève, MSS. 2344, 2349, 2351). In French tablature, the manuscripts contain pieces with such titles as, 'Branle de St. Nicolas', 'Branle de la musette', 'Ballet des Marmousets', 'Pantalonade', etc.

French court music and guitar styles spread, of course, to other countries as well. The beautiful manuscript of French guitar music made for Isabel van Langenhove, dated 1635, can still be found in Holland (Amsterdam, University Library). And the collection compiled by Johann Casper von Döremberg (East Berlin, Deutsche Staatsbibliothek, MS. 40142), was one of the first to be found in Germany. Later, French styles and French tablature were to dominate in all of the German-speaking countries.

In the 1650s, Francesco Corbetta made his first appearance at the court of the guitar-playing King Louis XIV in Paris, and made an instantaneous impact on both the King and his fellow court musicians. In the 1660s he left for England and the court of yet another guitar-playing francophile, King Charles II, where he was also spectacularly well received. And in about 1670 he returned to Paris (having himself by this time changed from Italian to French tablature),[22] and found that, as a result of his initial impact in the 1650s, a veritable 'French School' of guitar players and composers had developed during his absence.

François Martin published his little book of two guitar suites in 1663; this was followed in 1666 by Guillaume-Gabriel Nivers's tutor for voice and guitar. From this point onwards, we see a steady stream of French guitar music being published:

[22]Starting with his 1671 book; all his previous books were in Italian tablature.

F. Martin – 1663

G. Nivers – 1666, 1696

A. Carré – 1671, c.1675 (and another anonymous work which may well be his, c.1675)

R. Médard – 1676

H. Grénerin – 1680

R. de Visée – 1682, 1686

N. Derosier – 1688, 1690, 1696, 1699

F. Campion – 1705, 1730

When Corbetta died in 1681, his position in the court of Louis XIV was taken by his most famous pupil, Robert de Visée (c.1660–c.1724). De Visée's music is some of the most polished and refined of the period, the very epitome of elegance and sophistication, as exemplified by his piece, written on the death of his teacher, entitled 'Tombeau de M. Francisque Corbett'.

De Visée's music is perhaps the best known of the early guitar repertoire, and interest in his work has reached such an advanced stage that there are now facsimile editions of his two printed tablature books,[23] as well as a modern transcription which represents the contents of these books without distortion.[24]

For manuscript sources, one of the earliest, and certainly one of the most important, is a collection by various members of the De Gallot family (Oxford, Bodleian Library, Mus. Sch. c94), the pieces within ranging in date from c.1660 to c.1684.[25] It is an enormous source, containing over five hundred pieces from both the French and English courts, by such composers as Corbetta (it is a major source of his music), Dufaut,[26] de Gallot d'Irlande, de Gallot d'Angleterre, two other Gallots, a Mr Talbot, Arkangelo (Corelli?), and others. Many of the pieces are of the highest quality, comparing favourably with the best lute music of the same period. Of special interest is the inclusion of several guitar duos, trios, and pieces for 'guitthare theorbee', a five-course guitar with an extension for seven open basses. All in all, this source of music should top the list of anyone seriously wishing to explore the French school of guitar music.

The Bibliothèque Nationale in Paris also has several manuscripts of French guitar music from this period, including three containing a great many solos and *contreparties* (second guitar duet parts) by de Visée (Rés. F.844; Rés. 1402; Vm. ⁷6222). Another contains pieces by the lutenists Ennemond Gaultier and René Mesangeau (Vm. ⁷675).

[23]Minkoff Reprint (Geneva, 1973).
[24]'Strizich, V.
[25]I am indebted to Donald Gill for first bringing this MS. to my attention. Mr Gill has published a study of it in *Early Music*, Vol. 6, No. 1 (Jan. 1978).
[26]Two pieces by him from this MS. are published in modern edition with tablature; see Souris, D., pp. 97–98.

And a fifth manuscript is by François Campion, dated 1731 (Vm. ⁷6221).

Almost all of this music, except that of de Visée, is as yet unknown to modern musicians, and what appears to have been a genuine school of French guitarists (colleagues and contemporaries of Marin Marais and Jean-Baptiste Lully), awaits your serious attention.

Other sources, originating from this school, but found in other parts of Europe, are the 'Recueil des pièces de guitarre' of François Le Cocq (Brussels, Conservatoire, MS. 5615) dated 1729, which is a large and fine collection containing much French and Italian music; the guitar pieces by Count Logy von Losinthal (Prague, University, ii Kk77), dated late seventeenth century; and the extensive collection of solos, songs, duets, and ensemble pieces by Nathaniel Diesel in Copenhagen (Royal Library, Saml. 110 and 377), dating from between 1736 and 1744.[27]

THE 'SPANISH SCHOOL'

Published music for the five-course guitar in Spain begins with Juan Carlos Amat's book of 1596, and, ironically, virtually ends with a final reprint of that book c.1800! Here is a list of guitar books published in Spain or Naples between those two dates:

J. C. Amat – [1596], 1626, 1627, [1639], 1745, c.1750, 1752, 1758, c.1763, c.1780

N. Doizi de Velasco – 1640, [1645]

G. Sanz – 1674, 1675 (five editions), 1697 (two editions), [1791]

L. Ruiz de Ribayaz – 1677

F. Guerau – 1694

S. de Murcia – 1714

P. Minguet y Yrol – c.1752, 1774

A. de Sotos – 1764

Amat's modest little book with its chord system in 'Catalan'-style number notation has already been discussed, as have the simple chord pieces in Briçeño's book. The book by Andrés de Sotos is a tutor based upon Amat's, and the one by Pablo Minguet y Yrol is a collection of tutors for several instruments, the guitar tutor relying heavily, again, on Amat, and on Gaspar Sanz. There is little music in it: a few *alfabeto* pieces and seven quite charming but brief pieces in *punteado* style.

Nicolao Doizi de Velasco, a Portuguese in the service of Philip IV of Spain, published his extensive treatise on the guitar in 1640. It is actually the first really detailed and comprehensive instruction book for the guitar, which teaches theory, intabulating, stringing and tuning.

[27]See Lyons, D.

For the first publication of a collection of music, we turn to Gaspar Sanz, one of the few early guitarists about whom we have a fair bit of information. We know, for example, that he was born in 1640 in the tiny town of Calenda near Saragossa into an old and very well-to-do family; that he attended the University of Salamanca as a student of theology, but subsequently decided to pursue a career in music, for which he travelled to Italy, first to Naples where he became an organist in the Royal Chapel, and then to Rome, where he began his study of the guitar. Sanz's teacher was Lelio Colista, a prolific composer whose instrumental pieces were the direct models for those of Corelli and Purcell. It was also as a guitar student in Rome that Sanz met and studied the works of such great guitarists as Foscarini, Granata, and Corbetta, the latter being 'the best of all', according to Sanz.

After returning to his native Spain, he published his own book in 1674, which remains today a source of some of the most delightful music of its kind. In it, Sanz recommends the type of re-entrant tuning used by Briçeño, and implies that most of the Italian guitarists used it. Sanz's music provides us with a wide range of Spanish and Italian popular pieces, fine settings of *passacalles*, as well as preludes, pavans, etc.

But the treatment Sanz's music has received at the hands of modern editors presents a serious drawback to its revival. Because the modern listener has, over the years, become accustomed to hearing modern 'transcriptions' of several of his pieces, such as settings of the widely popular *canarios*, 'transcriptions' which make a feature of the booming basses of the modern guitar, it is bound to be difficult for him to adjust his ears to the sound of these pieces when they are played for him as they were meant to be played, on the light, delicate, alto-range instrument for which they were written. One hopes it will not be too many years before the music which Sanz *actually* wrote, sounding the way Sanz meant it to sound, finally becomes acceptable to the modern ear.[28]

Another interesting treatise and collection (though the printing of the music is atrocious) is Lucas Ruiz de Ribayaz's *Luz y norte musical* . . . of 1677, which is a veritable storehouse of extremely valuable information on the guitar, its technique and ornamentation.[29] Together with some of his own pieces in the collection, found at the end of the book, Ribayaz presents us with a selection of Gaspar Sanz's pieces, which have been altered for use on a guitar with *bourdons* on the fourth and fifth courses. He leaves out all the sections of Sanz's pieces which use the special idioms requiring the re-entrant tuning, and thus has the dubious distinction of being the forerunner of modern editors who similarly distort Sanz's music today.

[28]We are fortunate that a facsimile edition of his tablatures is now available (see Appendix 4). A non-distorted modern transcription of Sanz's works, edited by Robert Strizich, with tablatures, is soon to be published by Schott & Co., London, and the first part of a complete transcription, edited by Rodrigo de Zayas, appeared in *Guitar Review*, No. 40, (1976).
[29]See Strizich, R.

For music which was originally written for a guitar with *bourdons*, we can turn to the highly polished works of Francisco Guerau, whose 1694 book consists of *passacalles* in every key (comprising the major portion of the book), and settings of popular pieces such as *Xacaras, Mari-Zapolos, Marionas*, and *Canarios*. Guerau's speciality seems to have been composing variations on the themes of his material, and most of the pieces have quite extensive, varied repeats. His book is one of the rare guitar books of the seventeenth century which does not employ any strummed chords, all the music being notated entirely in the *punteado* style.[30]

Santiago de Murcia provides us with both a printed book, published in 1714, and a manuscript from 1732 (British Library, Add. 31640), each containing some of the very best five-course guitar music. Murcia is a master of the finely wrought suite. His basic material is very different from his predecessors', for, instead of using the popular Spanish tunes as, for example, Sanz did, his suites often consisted of a prelude, *allemand, courant, sarabande, gigue, gavotte*, etc. He was, in other words, influenced by the French school, which was new to Spain, and used the modified re-entrant tuning employed by Corbetta and de Visée, like them making frequent use of strummed chords.

There are a reasonable number of manuscript collections from Spanish writers to complement the printed works. Important among them are those by Antonio de Santa Cruz (Madrid, Biblioteca Nacional, MS. M.2209, c.1650), who, incidentally, calls the five-course guitar the 'biguela hordinaria' (common *vihuela*); one by Manuel Valero (Saragossa, Cathedral Library, c.1700); and a *Metodo de guitarra*, translated by Joseph Trapero (Madrid, Biblioteca Nacional, MS. 1233, c.1763).

Also of special interest is a Portuguese collection for 'viola' by Joseph Carneyro (Coimbra, MS. 97, c.1650), and three manuscripts from Mexico, one a cittern tutor, c.1650, which also contains some guitar music (San Pedro de los Pinos, Saldívar Collection); a mixed tablature collection with many native items (Mexico City, National Library, MS. 1560, early eighteenth century); and another similar one from the mid-eighteenth century (San Pedro de los Pinos, Saldívar Collection).

Spanish composers also figured in the movement for a new style guitar which began at the end of the eighteenth century.

THE CHANGE OF STYLE

The music for the five-course guitar so far discussed can be regarded as the 'classic' repertoire for the late renaissance and baroque instrument. On the whole, this music called for the characteristic re-entrant tunings, which were so important to the styles and idioms of the period, and which rendered the baroque guitar so unique an

[30]This volume is now available in an excellent facsimile edition with the text translated into English, published by Tecla Editions, London.

instrument.

Musical styles changed, however, and the development of these new styles – the Rococo and the Classical – with their simpler but stricter handling of chords, more efficient progressions (or modulations), and regularization of phrasing supported by clear key structure, meant that the guitar, too, had to become a more straightforwardly tuned instrument. It was no accident that around 1750, the guitar changed completely into an instrument with *bourdons* on the fourth and fifth courses, and later, to a six-course instrument.

The *bourdon* tuning, as we have seen, was nothing new; but, whereas previously it was the exception in art music, it now became the rule.

The first signs of this different way of thinking about the guitar occurred in France, where the instrument was enjoying yet another new wave of popularity. A flood of publications of songs accompanied by the guitar (and requiring a strong bass), appeared at this time, exemplified by De Lagarde's *Recueil de Brunettes . . .* (1751-1764). In the April issue of his *Journal de Musique*, De Lagarde made the following remark about one of the song accompaniments in tablature: 'Un bourdon à l'octave feroit mieux pour cet accompaniment' ('A *bourdon* at the octave [below] would be better for this accompaniment', p. 24). In a short time, this suggestion would no longer need mentioning.

Along with this developing emphasis on the bass range of the guitar, and the consequent abandonment of re-entrant tunings, notation began to change as well. Tablature, which was essential to reading music with a re-entrant tuning, became rarer; and guitar music appeared more and more frequently in more or less the modern printed form (i.e. in the treble clef with the notes sounding an octave lower). As we now know how the guitar developed its bass range, notation for it in the treble clef seems illogical and is often awkward to play from, but the choice of the treble clef is an interesting one and probably stems from the guitar's having been a higher ranged instrument in the past.[31] Nevertheless, and despite its awkwardness, the system was adopted, and apparently nothing can be done to change it.

The following list illustrates the increasing number of publications for the five-(double) course guitar with *bourdons*. As in the previous lists, it includes only sources which contain at least some solo music, and it does not include the numerous books of songs with guitar accompaniment. Most of the following use staff notation.

Anonymous (*Méthode pour . . . la guitarre*) – c.1760, c.1800

M. Corrette – 1763

E. Albanese – c.1770

A. Bailleux – 1773

[31] An early linking of the guitar to the treble clef is found in Matteis's 1682 book, in which he shows how the guitarist can read violin music, but sounding an octave lower.

P. Baillon – 1781

F. Alberti – 1786

A. M. Lemoine – 1790

B. Vidal – c.1790, c.1795, c.1797

P. Porro – c.1793, c.1800

L. Guichard – c.1795

G. Gatayes – c.1797, c.1798

In addition, there are several undated prints from this period, such as those by J. A. Amon and P. Aubert. The Italian names in the list indicate the emigration of a number of Italian guitarists to France. In fact, the five-course guitar with *bourdons* had become so established in France by the end of the seventeenth century, that the Italians commonly referred to it as the 'chitarra Francese'.[32]

The five courses of the guitar were not always just double; sometimes the fourth and fifth courses were triple as well. Michel Corrette's tutor (Paris, 1763), illustrates the stringing of 'guitarres à la Rodrigo' (see example 9a), and the Portuguese, Manuel da

Plate 10

Manuel da Paixaõ Ribeiro: *Nova arte de viola* (1789) (Estampa 1).

[32]For example, in Giuseppe Aprile, *Sei canzoncine con accompagnemento di chitarra francese* (Naples, 1792). There is a copy in the library of Robert Spencer.

Paixaõ Ribeiro shows us the stringing of the guitar (*viola*, in Portuguese), which he considers normal (example 9b and Plate 10). Notice in both cases that the stringing calls for the upper octave strings to be placed in the 'outer' position, that is, so that the thumb strikes the thinner strings of the fifth and fourth courses first.

Ex. 9

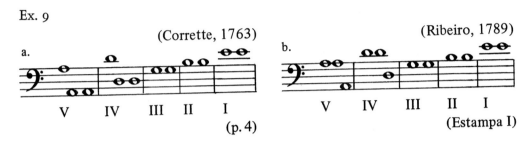

In England, at precisely the time of the rise of the new-style guitar in France (c.1750), many publications began to appear for the 'guittar' (as it was often spelled). But the 'English' guitar for which this music was written, is an entirely different instrument from the one we have been discussing, having six courses of *metal* strings with a chordal tuning. This instrument will be dealt with briefly later.

Also published in England was Francesco Chabran's *Compleat instructions for the Spanish guitar . . .* (c.1795), which was, of course, for the 'old' style, five-course guitar.[33] Five-course Spanish guitars were possibly made in the London workshops of John Preston in the late eighteenth century (Plate 11), but it wasn't until the early nineteenth century, the time of Louis Panormo (who made the new-style guitars with six single strings), that the Spanish guitar regained the popularity which it had, from the eighteenth century, lost to the 'English' guitar in England.

The first appearance of music for the six-course instrument was in 1780, Antonio Ballestero's *Obra para guitarra de seis ordenes*. This requires double courses tuned:

Ex. 10

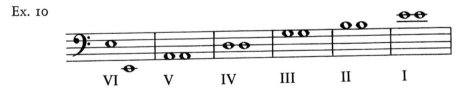

Ferandière and Rubio used this same arrangement in 1799, and it appears to be a Spanish development. Certainly, the guitars of the famous contemporary Spanish maker, Juan

[33]Chabran's tuning instructions are vague, and they could possibly imply a guitar (e¹ tuning) with five *single* strings. Robert Spencer owns a later edition (1807?) which requires a guitar of six single strings.

Plate II
Late eighteenth-century guitar signed: 'Preston London' on label inside. (*Author's collection.*)

Photo: Tom Evans

Pages, would bear out this premise.[34] Although many of his guitars were later converted to hold six single strings, the Pages, and most other Spanish-made guitars of this time, were originally designed to hold twelve strings arranged in six double courses.

Other Spanish books for the six-course guitar are:

F. Moretti – [1792], 1799, c.1800

A. Abreu – 1799

F. Ferandière – 1799

J. Rubio – 1799

The double-course guitar in Spain lasted until well into the 1830s, as some of the surviving instruments prove, but the trend to six single strings was rapidly growing.

In France, as Robert Spencer has pointed out to me, the first appearance of music for the six-course instrument was in 1785, a song accompaniment calling for a 'guitarre portant une corde de plus'.[35] France also seems to have been the birthplace of a new instrument at this time, the lyre (see Grunfeld, A., Plate 133), an instrument which combined the appearance of the ancient Greek lyre with the modern practicality of a guitar finger-board. This was apparently a product of the 'Classical revival' which was taking place in the late eighteenth century.[36] Most examples carry from six to nine single strings, and this feature may have had an influence on the guitar's changing to six single strings. Lemoine's *Nouvelle Methode* (1790), for instance, includes the use of a guitar with five single strings, six single strings, and the lyre.[37]

Our history of the double-course guitar ends here, for although the instrument lingered on for a while longer, the modern guitar emerged quickly at the beginning of the nineteenth century.

To summarize Chapters 2 and 3, we have seen how the guitar in the fifteenth century was very soon distinguished from the larger *viola*, or *vihuela*, and how this small treble instrument developed a role and a repertoire all its own in the sixteenth century. We have seen how, by the seventeenth century, the larger five-course instrument took the lead and developed, with its special tunings, into a unique and distinguished instrument with a repertoire and character quite unlike that which modern players have tended to project onto it; that only from about 1750 did the nature of the

[34]There is a six-course guitar by Joachim Tielke in London (Victoria and Albert Museum, No. 676–1872) with eleven pegs (single first and double remaining courses), dating from about 1700. However, the single extra peg, merely added at the top of the peghead, and the change of bridge, could easily have been done at a later date. The likelihood of this easy conversion and the weight of evidence points to its having been a normal five-course guitar at the time of its original construction. (See Baines, E., No. 292.)

[35]Anon., *Etrennes de Polymnie* . . . (Paris, 1785, p. 148). The guitar part going down to G is in staff notation. A copy of the book is in the library of Robert Spencer.

[36]See Bonner, C.

[37]There is a facsimile edition by Minkoff (Geneva, 1977).

guitar change, and did it begin to approach the instrument we know today. We have learned that these changes in the guitar were the result of changes in style and approaches to music; that the modern instrument is not the result of an unbroken 'development' and the quest for 'perfection', but simply a tool which reflects our current approach to music, an approach which, like all others in the past, will also change. By studying the instruments, styles, and playing techniques of the past, we can discover the many useful ideas which have until now been lost to us, and which, regained, can refresh, invigorate, and, I hope for many, point to directions for the future.

PART TWO
HANDBOOK

4

TUNING AND STRINGING

The following is a résumé of the three main tunings of the five-course guitar:

Ex. 11

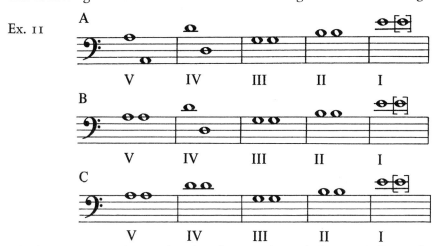

The list of sources (Appendix 1) will carry the code letters A, B, or C next to each individual item to indicate which tuning applies (provided I am reasonably sure which does apply !). Tuning B is the one most frequently used in seventeenth-century art music. Four-course music, played entirely solo, can be played on the top four courses of the five-course instrument (tuning B), but if a proper four-course guitar is available, it should be tuned as follows:

Ex. 12

Since the guitar's earliest days, gut strings have been used on it. These were plain strings of different thicknesses, and, even when overspun or wound strings came into use in the second half of the seventeenth century, most players continued to use plain gut strings. Modern nylon strings are a reasonable substitute for gut, for, although nylon sounds rather flabby at the low tensions required on early guitars as compared to the bright sound of gut, nylon does have the advantage of being readily available and lower in price. The use of gut, however, is becoming increasingly popular amongst players using instruments built following historical principles, and an excellent introduction to gut stringing (and its problems), is the article by Djilda Abbott and Ephraim Segerman, 'Gut Strings.'[1]

Whichever one chooses, gut or nylon, it is essential that the strings be much thinner than those used on a modern guitar. The average first string of a modern guitar, for example, would serve for the second of an early guitar. Should the thinner nylon strings be required, however, the lute strings mass-produced by such firms as Pyramid are of sufficient thinness to serve.

Upon stringing up an early guitar, it is advisable to put the upper octave string of the fourth course (and fifth for tuning A), in the 'outside' position where the thumb would strike the upper string before it strikes the *bourdon*. This enables one to play just the upper string alone when necessary (in, for example, a *campanella* passage), or both strings together when a bass is needed. Many of the seemingly ambiguous passages in some of the tablatures become clear when one realizes that a choice of notes can be played on the fourth course.[2]

For this method of stringing, we have no less an authority than Antonio Stradivari, who, in his surviving writings, gives a clear stringing table for tuning B.[3] He also mentions that the strings of the third course must be the thick, gut, first strings of the violin.

Many European, English, and American instrument makers and string suppliers advertise in the pages of the journal *Early Music*,[4] and the names and addresses of these and other makers and dealers, some of whom will also give advice on strings and stringing, appear in the same journal's *Register of Early Instruments and Makers*.

For the guitarist working with a modern instrument, there is a choice of selecting music in the list of sources (Appendix 1) marked for tuning A, in which case the first five strings can be used as they stand, or the sources marked for tuning C, with which a first string can replace the fourth and a second string can replace the fifth. For music using tuning B, one can often satisfactorily use tuning C, but not A. As a temporary measure, a lightly constructed twelve-string guitar can be re-strung with nylon, and, because of the double courses, any of the above tunings can be used. Needless to say, I would strongly encourage anyone who seriously intends to study and perform early guitar music to obtain an historically accurate instrument.

[1]Abbott and Segerman, G.

[2]It is advisable to arrange the octave strings on the four-course instrument in this manner as well, for the choice of upper or lower notes would eliminate many of the curious second inversion chords one encounters in the tablatures for this instrument, particularly at cadences.

[3]See Frizoli, S., p. 40. The Diderot and D'Alembert *Encyclopédie* (1757 edition), in the entry 'Guitarre', gives a chart on p. 1013 which clearly shows this form of stringing for tuning A.

[4]Oxford University Press, Ely House, 37 Dover Street, London W1X 4AH, England.

5

TABLATURE

For anyone taking a practical interest in the early guitar, the ability to read tablature, the special notation for all early plucked instruments, is absolutely essential. All guitar music dating from the sixteenth century right up to the late eighteenth century was notated in tablature, a basically simple and straightforward system, the success and practicality of which are demonstrated by the length of time it continued in use.

There are many advantages in being able to read tablature. First, it reflects as closely as possible the composer's intentions, a detail too often ignored today in the performance of early music. Secondly, the ability to read it frees the player from having to rely totally on the few and often distorted versions of early guitar music found in modern editions. And thirdly, it offers a very efficient, time-and-space-saving method for notating music; unlike staff notation, with which the player reads a pitch and then must interpret where on the instrument to place his fingers, tablature simply *tells* him where!

ITALIAN TABLATURE

As most of the important early guitar music was written by Italian and Spanish composers, it is appropriate to begin with their system.

The five-line staff below represents the five courses of the guitar (the first four lines for a four-course guitar), and numbers placed on or between the lines represent the frets to be used: o=open string, 1=first fret, 2=second fret, 3=third fret, etc. For the tenth, eleventh, and twelfth frets, x, ii, and 12 are used.

Ex. 13

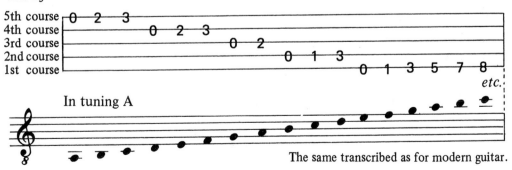

The same transcribed as for modern guitar.

The rhythm signs, usually ordinary, free-standing notes, are placed over the staff above the appropriate numbers; these show when each note or chord (represented by the tablature number), begins. The duration of any individual note depends on technical factors, such as how long the left-hand finger can remain holding it until it is necessary to move it to play another note. It is assumed that bass notes will be held for as long as possible. The value of the rhythm sign remains valid until a new sign appears.

Ex. 14

For the right hand, the only notated signs are single dots under individual notes, particularly in running scale passages. These dots indicate that the note is to be played with the index finger. In later seventeenth-century music, two dots under a note indicate that the middle finger is to be used.

Only five- and four-course tablature, specifically for the guitar, is illustrated here, but the same system and principles also apply for lute and *vihuela* tablatures; merely add a sixth line to represent the sixth course.

FRENCH TABLATURE

This system differs from the Italian in the following ways: (a) While the courses of the guitar are still indicated by five (or four) lines, they are in the reverse order thus:

Ex. 15

1st course	——————————
2nd course	——————————
3rd course	——————————
4th course	——————————
5th course	——————————

(b) Instead of numbers to indicate the frets, letters are used in the following fashion: a=open string, b=first fret, c=second fret, d=third fret, etc. Note that the letter 'j' did not yet exist at this time, hence the sequence runs . . . g, h, i, k, l, etc.

Ex. 16

(c) The rhythm signs are often indicated by the following figures:

Ex. 17

Ex. 17 (cont.)

As with the Italian system, the values of the rhythm signs remain valid for all subsequent notes until a new sign appears.

A knowledge of the foregoing information is sufficient to cope with the majority of straight *punteado* (lute style) tablatures, such as sixteenth-century Spanish music for guitar and *vihuela* and early French music for the four-course guitar. But tablatures for later seventeenth- and eighteenth-century guitar music also require a knowledge of various additional signs for ornaments, and of technical considerations which will be dealt with in succeeding chapters.

THE GUITAR 'ALFABETO' SYSTEM

The Italian chord system known as *alfabeto* was by far the most widely used, and, as most of the major composers for the early guitar employed it, either alone or mixed in with the previously discussed *punteado* tablature, it is essential to learn it.

The idea of the system is to assign a specific symbol or letter of the alphabet to one specific chord. With a few exceptions, the chord involves all five courses of the instrument, which is strummed in a variety of ways (see TECHNIQUE and THE ORNAMENTS).

Graphically, the system is as follows:

Ex. 18

Ex. 18 (cont.)

O	P	Q	R	S	T	V	X	Y	Z	&	?	Ry
1	3	4	2	2	4	4	2	5	3	4	2	3
0	3	4	4	2	2	4	4	5	5	3	2	3
0	1	3	4	4	2	2	4	4	5	1	4	5
3	1	2	4	5	2	2	3	3	5	2	5	6
3	1	2	2	4	5	5	2	3	3	1	3	4

Note that the letters have no relationship to the actual harmonic name of the chord as in our modern system; they are purely symbols. Notice also that some of the chords use the same finger pattern, but in a higher position. For this reason some *alfabeto* books offer a simpler modification in which a number is put over the basic chord pattern to show the position to which the fingers should be shifted. Here, for example, are chords in the third and fifth positions:

Ex. 19

G3	G5	H3	H5	M3	M5	N3	N5
5	7	3	5	3	5	5	7
5	7	5	7	3	5	3	5
4	6	5	7	5	7	3	5
3	5	5	7	6	8	3	5
3	5	3	5	5	7	6	8

Further refinements include Foscarini's 'alfabeto dissonante', in which the basic chord is changed to include a dissonance or suspension:

Ex. 20

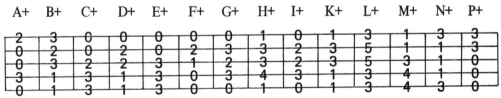

A+	B+	C+	D+	E+	F+	G+	H+	I+	K+	L+	M+	N+	P+
2	3	0	0	0	0	0	1	0	1	3	1	3	3
0	2	0	2	0	2	3	3	2	3	5	1	1	3
0	3	2	2	3	1	2	3	2	3	5	3	1	0
3	1	3	1	3	0	3	4	3	1	3	4	1	0
0	1	3	1	3	0	0	1	0	1	3	4	3	0

and Calvi's 'alfabeto falso', for a different arrangement of dissonances:

Ex. 21

A*	B*	C*	D*	E*	F*	G*	H*	I*	L*	N*	O*	P*
0	3	0	0	0	0	0	1	0	3	1	0	3
0	3	0	2	3	2	3	3	2	1	1	0	1
0	0	2	2	2	1	2	3	2	0	1	2	2
0	1	1	0	3	0	1	4	3	4	1	3	1
3	0	2	0	0	0	0	1	0	3	3	3	1

also, Ricci's 'lettere tagliate':

Ex. 22

```
        At    Ct    Dt    Et
        0     0     0     0
        0     0     2     0
        0     2     2     2
        3     3     0     3
        3     0     0     0
```

Different inversions and positions of the same basic chord are called by Millioni 'lettere false'.

Some *alfabeto* diagrams simply present the frets to be fingered and leave the remaining tablature lines blank. The blank lines mean that those strings are to be played open; thus all five courses are, under normal circumstances, played for each symbol. The occasional exceptions to the rule will be described later.

Once the *alfabeto* system has been memorized (at least up to the letter 'H'), the next step is to investigate how the chords are put together rhythmically. The usual method was to use a single horizontal line, often divided off into bars, with the *alfabeto* letters placed above or below. Short vertical lines were then placed on the horizontal, a line hanging down meaning that the chord was to be strummed with a down stroke (i.e. the right hand travels in the direction of the floor, striking the fifth to the first courses in that order), and a line above meaning the opposite. When playing just *alfabeto* material, the right hand should be placed near the junction of the neck with the body of the guitar, as recommended by several of the early writers. A time signature appears at the beginning (3=triple metre, C or ₵=duple metre) and, frequently, rhythmic values appear over the appropriate notes. To illustrate, an 'Aria detta del Gran Duca' from Sanseverino's 1620 book:

Ex. 23

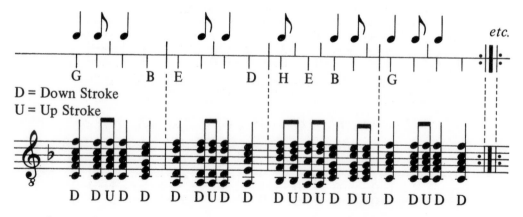

D = Down Stroke
U = Up Stroke

(*Note:* The inversions of the chords will be different with tunings 'B' and 'C'.)

Although the foregoing *alfabeto* is by far the most common, certain individual writers vary the system by changing one or two small details, so, when working with any of the early guitar books, avoid unnecessary confusion by always studying the *alfabeto* diagram, which is generally printed at the beginning of each book, before proceeding to the music (Plate 12).

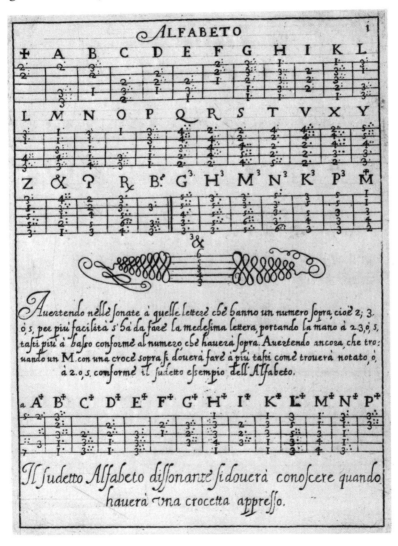

Plate 12
Foscarini (c.1632), p.1.

Sometimes, the *alfabeto* books are quite vague in their presentation of pieces, giving neither rhythm signs nor barlines. As an aid to deciding how to transcribe these pieces, Johannes Wolf[1] devised the following theoretical table:

Ex. 24

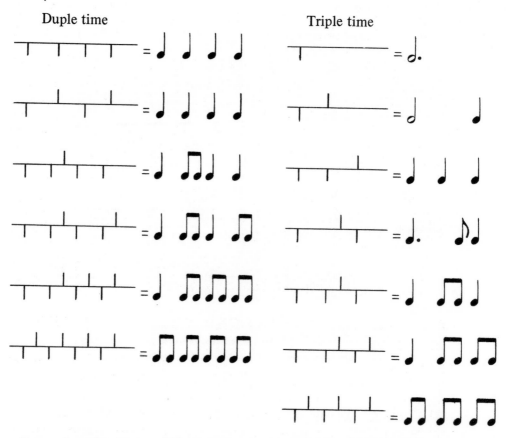

For an introduction to *alfabeto* music, the books by Sanseverino (1620) and Calvi (1646) are recommended for their relative clarity of presentation. (A considerable number of books containing only solo *alfabeto* music are included in the list of sources in Appendix 1 (Plate 13).)

In addition to the books of solo *alfabeto* music, there are also many song books which include *alfabeto* chords to accompany the voice. In these, the letters are placed over the music in a manner strikingly similar to the notating of guitar chords on modern sheet music. Sometimes the song books give only a printed text with the *alfabeto* letters over

[1]Wolf, H., pp. 179-180.

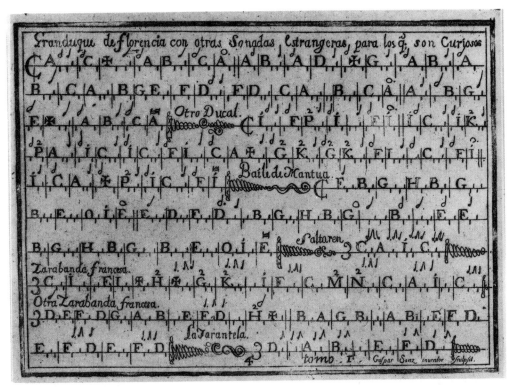

Plate 13
Examples of *alfabeto* pieces from Gaspar Sanz: *Instruccion* (1674), f.19. For a transcription
see Zayas, C., pp.21–27.

the appropriate words. Since these books generally contain the well-known, popular
songs of the day, their publishers apparently did not feel it was necessary to print the
tune as well. For those unfamiliar with the 'pop charts' of the seventeenth century,
however, a knowledge of the songs from other sources is necessary before full use can
be made of these books. Of course, there are numerous song books with the tune and
even a figured bass included. These, however, do not contain popular songs, but 'art'
songs. A typical 'art' song book is *Le musiche del Sigismondo d'India a una e due voci da
cantarsi nel chitarrone . . . con alcune arie, con l'alfabeto per la chitarra alla spagnola . . .* (1621).

As well as songs, the guitar often accompanied instrumental chamber music. The
method of indicating the accompaniment was to place the *alfabeto* letters over the staff
notation in the same manner as for *alfabeto* song accompaniments. Biagio Marini's
Diversi generi do sonate da chiesa e da camera, libro iii, Op. 22 (1655), provides some good
examples of this form of accompaniment. (See the list of sources in Appendix 1 for the
locations of these and other books of a similar nature.)

Other systems of *alfabeto* notation, using numbers for symbols, seem to be entirely Spanish in origin and in use. These are the 'Castilian' system, used by Briçeño and Ribayaz, and the 'Catalan' system, used by Amat and Minguet. As there are very few books and manuscripts which employ these systems, it will suffice to simply present contemporary diagrams by way of explaining them.

The 'Castilian' system is beautifully illustrated by Briçeño, who, in his 1626 book, presents the chords (*puntos*) in French tablature and places the numbers and other signs above their respective chords (Plate 14).

LOS PVNTOS O AQVERDOS.

DE LA GVITARRA.

Plate 14
L. Briçeño: *Metodo mui facilissimo* (1626), f. 4v.

Amat's 'Catalan' system is given in Minguet's 1774 book, in which twelve major and twelve minor chords, beginning with 1n (*natural*) to 12n, then 1b (*b molado*) to 12b are illustrated (Plate 15).

The Spanish systems were used in exactly the same way as the Italian *alfabeto*, the difference between them being only one of notation.

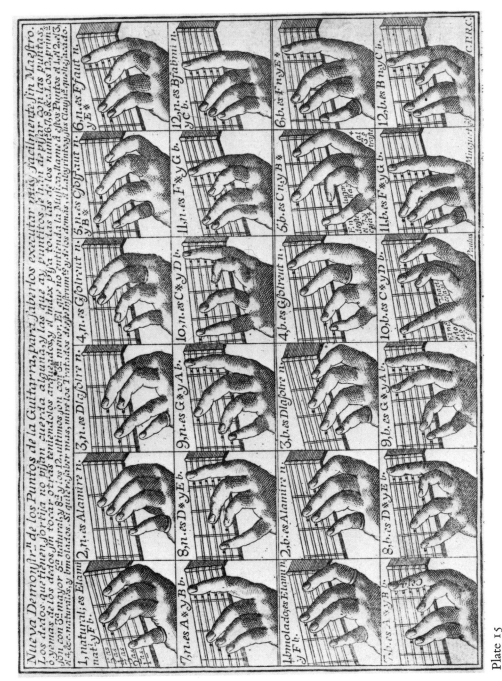

Plate 15

Minguet y Yrol: *Reglas y advertencias* (1774), plate 2–2.

MIXED TABLATURES

Having learned the *alfabeto*, the next area to be explored is that of mixed tablatures. These tablatures are of the common Italian type such as Fuenllana used in his 1554 book and Calvi in his 1646 book. However, for mixed tablatures, instead of a chord being written out in full, its *alfabeto* symbol was used within the regular lute-style tablature. The marks for up or down strokes are found directly below the symbol or slightly after it, and the note-heads for rhythm apply in the usual manner:

Ex. 25

Chords that do not fit into the *alfabeto* system are written out in full; these are to be played using only the specific notes indicated, not necessarily the full five courses of an *alfabeto* chord. Occasionally, you will find an example like the one below, which should be interpreted as a struck chord employing only the following four notes:

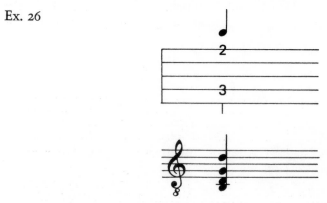

Ex. 26

To illustrate the mixed tablature style, here is a section from a *ciaccona* by Francesco Corbetta from his 1648 collection:

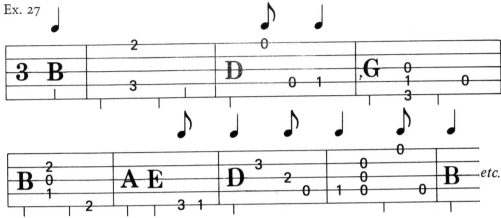

Ex. 27

Mixed tablatures appeared less frequently toward the end of the seventeenth century in Italy, and French tablature publications tended to do without the *alfabeto* system entirely, reverting back to fully written-out chords. In some French tablatures, such as those by Robert de Visée, the note-heads served both their normal rhythmic function, and, when placed inside the staff, served as an indication of the stroke required for the right-hand chords. For example, when the tail of the note-head hangs down, the chord after which it has been placed is meant to receive a full down stroke for the time value represented by the note-head. And the reverse: if the note-tail points upward, an up stroke of the right hand is required. Always be sure to distinguish between note-heads *above* the staff, which function in the standard tablature context, and note-heads *in* the staff after chords, which, in addition, show the right-hand stroke.

Often the common chords are written with only the fingerboard notes on the staff and the remaining lines left blank. Apparently, when a down or up stroke is also indicated, it is assumed that the blank lines are, nevertheless, to be played as open strings. For example:

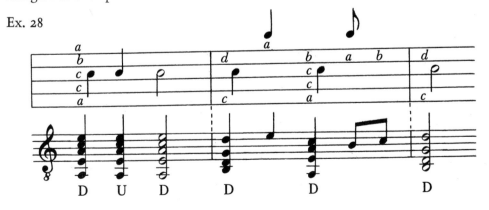

Ex. 28

75

Further, there are occasions when a strummed chord requires only four or three courses. In such cases, a dot will generally be found on the line or lines which are *not* to be played:

Ex. 29

When no dots appear, the player will have to decide for himself whether any of the courses are to remain silent. It goes without saying that the strum must be carefully and accurately executed so that the right-hand fingers do not strike the unwanted courses.

Finally, one small, additional point needs to be made concerning mixed tablatures. Sometimes, after a full *alfabeto* chord, there follows a single note which, nevertheless, has a stroke sign (usually an up stroke), under it. Most of the time this can be construed as a single note to be plucked with an up stroke of the right hand index finger (as though a dot instead of a stroke line was under the note). Occasionally, however, it could mean that the entire previous chord should be strummed again, adding the new note to the fabric of the chord. The earlier writers are rarely clear on these points, so, once again, it is the player's responsibility to decide what to do when such a note appears. When it does, it will look like this:

Ex. 30

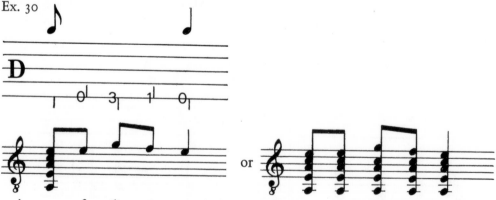

A survey of auxiliary signs, symbols for ornaments, and technical devices follows in the next two chapters.

6

TECHNIQUE

Owing to the vagueness of early guitar composers about playing technique, lute and *vihuela* technique must be the basis for that of the early guitar. Still, given that: (a) the first guitar music appears in the *vihuela* and lute books from Spain and Italy; (b) the early French guitar books were compiled by lute players such as Le Roy and Gorlier; and (c) many seventeenth-century guitarists such as Foscarini and de Visée also played the lute or theorbo, I think we can be fairly confident that a reasonably accurate picture of guitar technique can be gleaned from these *vihuela* and lute sources.

THE RIGHT HAND

There was nothing approaching a standard technique for the right hand, but two basic positions seem to have been used most often: the first, with the thumb 'inside' the fingers, was quite common in the sixteenth century (see Plate 2), and the second, with the thumb 'outside' the fingers, approaches the modern position (Plate 16).

The lutenist J. B. Bésard explained the matter thus:

> First of all, rest the little finger firmly on the belly of the lute, not very close to the rose (as they call it), but a little below it, and extend the thumb with the strength of the hand, especially if your hand is a little too short. Do this in such a way that the rest of the fingers are carried below the thumb in the manner of a fist. This will perhaps be a strain at first, and somewhat difficult. Those who have a very short thumb may imitate those who pluck the strings while hiding the thumb under the fingers; if not an elegant position, it will at least be easier. Having chosen one of these two methods, accustom yourself to plucking the strings, whether one or more, quite strongly and clearly.
>
> *Novus Partus*, 1617[1]

In both hand positions, the little finger is placed on the soundboard of the instrument to lend support and to provide a stable point from which to gauge the distances to the strings. The entire right hand is placed, approximately, between the rosette and the bridge.

[1]The translation is from Sutton, I., pp. 355-6.

Plate 16
R. Médard: *Pieces de Guitarre* (1676) (title page).

For music of the sixteenth and well into the seventeenth centuries, the thumb is meant to alternate with the index finger in single-line passage work on all the courses, treble to bass. Most lute and guitar books carefully notate this by placing a dot under the notes intended for the index finger; no dot means that the note is to be played with the thumb. For example:

Ex. 31

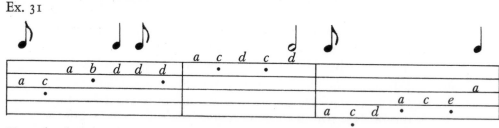

Since the thumb is, by nature, stronger than the index finger, the sound produced will be one of alternating strong and slightly weaker stresses. This articulation is carefully matched to the rhythm of the passage, and the result is an absolutely clear and natural emphasis of that rhythm. To the renaissance ear, these alternating stresses must have been important. Not only do the lute books indicate this, but many keyboard and wind instrument books also make a feature of it. This style of rhythmic articulation is very different from that of the modern guitarist, who is taught to make all the notes of equal stress in most passages. But to understand and to interpret early music accurately, the modern player must take these renaissance ideas seriously into account.[2]

The thumb and first finger method for single line work seems to be by far the most common. Second to it, was the alternation of the middle with the index fingers. Although the latter is mentioned in Fuenllana's *vihuela* book of 1554, it did not really come into common use until later, in the seventeenth century.

Fuenllana (f.5-6) mentions not only the thumb and index method, and the middle and index method, but also an intriguing third technique for playing single lines, the 'dedillo' stroke, which he describes as the rapid back and forth motion of the index finger alone, one stroke in either direction serving for one note of the passage.

For single lines with a second, usually a bass, line, the technique is much the same, except the thumb is needed to play the bass at the start of the passage. The middle finger, therefore, plays the initial note of the treble, while the thumb plays the bass. After the second treble note is played with the index, the thumb then jumps to the treble to continue the normal pattern. For later music, the middle finger often replaces the thumb in playing the treble. Here is an example which illustrates both methods:

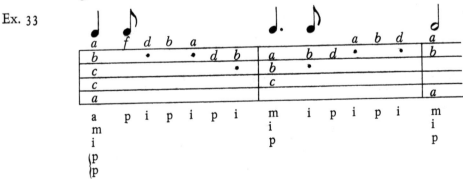

Ex. 32

p = Thumb
i = Index finger
m = Middle finger
a = Third finger

For chords, of course, the thumb, index, middle, and third fingers are all used, the thumb striking two courses when a five-note chord is required:

Ex. 33

²See Myers, V., p. 18.

Further illustrations of right-hand fingering can be seen in the facsimiles of tablatures included in this book.

An important subject which should be mentioned in conjunction with right-hand technique is fingernails. To my knowledge, the guitar books do not mention the use or non-use of nails in relation to right-hand technique, until the very end of the period we are concerned with here (c.f. Antonio Abreu, 1799). We must, therefore, once again base our decisions on the existing information found in lute sources, and, on the weight of these sources, the flesh technique must be acknowledged to be by far the most common. However, this does not mean that nails were never used.

Actual references to right-hand nails are indeed rare, the earliest being Fuenllana's in 1554. (His book, you will recall, also contained guitar music.) In speaking about the technique of playing rapid single line passages (*redobles*), he comments that he does not like the sound of the nail in the return motion of the *dedillo* stroke, and, in discussing the alternation of the middle and index finger style, he says: '. . . it is best by far to pluck the string using neither nail or any other device. Only the finger, the living thing, can communicate the intention of the spirit' (f.6). Despite his rejection of nail technique, Fuenllana's comments certainly do imply that some players did use nails.

In his 1623 lute and *chitarrone* book, Alessandro Piccinini[3] provides us with a great many fascinating technical details, considerably more than most writers. He advocates nails, saying that the one on the thumb should not be very long and that the others should be somewhat longer, coming just slightly above the fingertips and oval-shaped (i.e. the highest point should be in the middle of the nail). He also instructs the player to touch the course with the flesh and push the finger towards the belly, letting the nail glide over both strings of the course (Chapter 7).

Piccinini seems to be unique among lutenists in actually recommending the use of nails as a normal practice, but we should consider him carefully for several reasons: first, he stands as one historical justification for the fact that some lutenists did use nails; secondly, he was an important musician of his day; and thirdly, his name is mentioned, along with other musicians known to have been guitarists, in Granata's 1659 book.

In practice, a modern player attempting to play on a lightly-constructed, lightly-strung, double-strung, historically accurate instrument, will find that very long nails simply get in the way, especially the thumb nail. The bridge is very low on an original-style guitar, and because of this, there is even the practical problem of how to avoid marking the sound board of the instrument as one plays. If one is going to use nails, then the best approach is Piccinini's, i.e. very short ones. In order to avoid the annoying double sounding of each note which occurs when playing the double courses with nails, keep the hand in an oblique position so that the nails cross the strings diagonally. This

[3]See Buetens, I., pp. 6-17.

should at least serve to lessen the effect. This problem does not arise when one plays without nails, because the large soft area of the fingertip adequately touches both strings simultaneously.

Interestingly, there is a reference to Corbetta's using nails on the guitar in his later years. Corbetta is mentioned in the published memoirs of Adam Ebert (*Auli Apronii vermehrte Reise-Beschreibung . . .* 1723). Ebert remembers seeing Corbetta at Turin and writes: '. . . the world-famous guitarist Corbetta, who taught all the Potentates of Europe, came here from England. But because he had the misfortune to break a finger-nail (and with old folk these are accustomed to grow again very slowly) it was impossible for him to present himself at the festival with his consort. . . .'[4]

Two other lute sources mention the use of nails. One is a letter from 1723, written by the famous lutenist-friend of Bach's, Silvius Leopold Weiss. In it, Weiss indicates that the lute is usually played with the flesh, but the theorbo and *chitarrone* are usually played with nails 'and produce in close proximity a coarse, harsh sound.'[5]

The other lute source is Thomas Mace (1676), who lets us choose for ourselves: '. . . take notice, that you strike not your strings with your nails, as some do, who maintain it the best way of play, but I do not; and for this reason; because the nail cannot draw so sweet a sound from a lute, as the nibble end of the flesh can do. I confess in a consort, it might do well enough, where the mellowness (which is the most excellent satisfaction from a lute) is lost in the crowd; but alone, I could never receive so good content from the nail, as from the flesh: However (this being my opinion) let others do, as seems best to themselves.'

THE LEFT HAND

Early guitar sources leave the topic of left-hand fingering virtually blank, dealing only with the fingerings of the *alfabeto* chords, and giving the usual advice about keeping the left-hand fingers firmly down when playing a passage, removing them only when it becomes necessary to finger other notes. Lute books provide little more instruction. It would appear, however, that the principles of left-hand fingering are essentially similar to those found in present-day guitar tutors, and anyone who has had any classical guitar training at all will be able to apply it to the early guitar.

BATTENTE TECHNIQUE[6]

Returning to the right hand, there is another major area to examine: the strumming technique which the Italians termed *battente* and the Spanish, *rasgueado*. It is important

[4]R. T. Pinnell's translation in Pinnell, R., p. 256.
[5]See Smith, B., p. 52.
[6]See Murphy, R.

to realize that contrary to the disparaging and belittling viewpoint of modern writers regarding strumming and the earliest *alfabeto* books, this was a fundamental and unique feature of the guitar from its earliest history. The finest music of Corbetta, Sanz, and de Visée utilized both the strumming style and the *pizzicato* style.

Normally, all five of the courses are struck. The tablatures indicate when less are required. When playing passages entirely of full chords (as presented in the *alfabeto* books), the right hand is held so that the fingers are at the junction of the neck and body of the guitar. This is illustrated in several contemporary paintings and mentioned in several guitar books.[7] To make a down stroke ($\top$), i.e. from the fifth to the first course, one has the option of either playing with the single index finger (or the middle finger), or quickly rolling two or three fingers, brushing them in a slightly spread fashion over the five courses. Sometimes the thumb alone is used. The different methods each produce a different sound, a fact which should be taken into account when deciding which to use for a particular passage.

To play an up stroke ($\perp$), one most often uses the index finger alone, but in certain circumstances, such as to play a *repicco*, the thumb is also used. To play a stroke pattern such as B one can play either two downs with the index finger and the up also with the index fiinger; or two downs with the thumb and up with the index; or middle-thumb-index; middle-index-index; alternatively, one can brush the courses with three spread fingers for a quite different sound. (See also the *repicco* patterns described in THE ORNAMENTS.)

For playing mixed tablature, the right hand should be down in its usual place between the bridge and the rosette. The *pizzicato* notes should be played using the techniques described at the beginning of this chapter, and the *battente* chords, generally, in the same position. You will probably find that keeping the right hand near the bridge restricts its freedom of movement somewhat. You should, therefore, bring your hand back up to the neck whenever there is sufficient time to shift back and forth, or when there is an extended chord passage in the music. These are also the best times to do any of the intricate strumming patterns. Otherwise, in the lower position, it is ,best to keep the strokes simple, leaving the little finger on the soundboard of the instrument, as for *pizzicato* playing.

The early guitar composers allow us a great deal of freedom to elaborate on the rhythm patterns in chord passages, particularly in the solo *alfabeto* material. With skilled and practised performance, the results can be immensely exciting, and, in some cases, similar in nature to the opening of the Rodrigo Guitar Concerto, an extremely popular item with classical guitarists today.

[7]Millioni, 1627 (see Murphy, R., p. 27) and Mersenne, 1636.

7

THE ORNAMENTS

No ornament signs are found in guitar sources from the sixteenth century. This does not mean that ornaments were not played on the guitar at this time; quite the contrary. The reason why music in the printed books contained no ornament signs is probably to be found in the typographical difficulties involved. Later, with the appearance of engraved music books, this problem no longer existed. Despite this lack of early notated signs, we know that some ornaments, especially trills and mordents, were used often, for some writers, such as Bermudo in 1555, complain about players who add too many!

As a guide to the earlier ornaments, I have once again turned to contemporary lute sources. From the beginning of the seventeenth century, however, the guitar books themselves begin to supply us with information, and a whole range of added ornaments are described (although not as precisely perhaps as our modern needs might require). These occur in the two basic playing styles, the *battente* and the *pizzicato*.

BATTENTE STYLE (RASGUEADO)

The following ornaments are unique to this playing style and, indeed, to the guitar itself.

A. *Trillo*

This is a series of rapid down and up strokes described in various ways by contemporary guitarists.

> The trillo is made with the finger called the index, touching all the strings downwards and upwards with rapidity. . . .
>
> (Abbatessa, 1627, f.3)

> . . . when the player has had practice in moving his hand well and has learned the fingerboard of the guitar, and learned all the chords, it will then be necessary to vary the [right] hand with different kinds of *trillo* and *repicco*. And concerning the way of trilling is the advice that with the thumb and the middle finger [respectively] one makes the strokes. For example: A ⊤ which is made with a downward stroke with the thumb and then an up stroke [with the thumb] and similarly with

the middle finger [for the succeeding stroke sign]. This is the technique of this percussive ornament if a *trillo* is needed.

Note further that the *trillo* is also made with the index finger dividing the stroke into four parts, i.e. into four quavers if there is a minim. The first down, the second up, the third down, and the fourth up. But all these should be made with a speed corresponding to the tempo of the piece.   (Foscarini, c.1630, f.4)

Foscarini, then, tells us to play two strokes to every one that is printed and gives us the choice as to when to use the *trillo*. One style of playing these strokes is the following:

The four strokes should be bound together in a winding fashion like a wheel. . . .   (Ricci, 1677, p.13)

This seems very like the 'S' or 'windmill' stroke used by the modern banjoist and ukulele player!

B. *Repicco*

The *repicco* is similar to the *trillo*, but is often much more complicated and, as a result, has more rhythmic vitality.

To play a *repicco* one plays four strokes, i.e. two down and two up. The first down is played with the middle finger, the second down with the thumb, the third up is played with the thumb and the fourth up with the index, playing however only the first course. A *repicco* lasts for two [printed] strokes [⊤⊥].[1]   (Pico, 1608)

This is the basic four-stroke pattern, which, like that of the *trillo*, doubles the number of printed strokes in the same amount of time. With the thumb brought into play, however, the actual sound and stresses of the two ornaments are quite different.

The *repicco* is made with [two][2] fingers; the index or middle and the thumb which touches all the strings downwards and returns rapidly upward.   (Abbatessa, 1627, f.3ᵛ)

This does not tell us much, but it is possible that Abbatessa is actually describing a variation of the four-stroke pattern – that is, a three-stroke pattern: thumb down, thumb up, index (or middle) up.

Various sorts of *picchi* and *repicchi* are made on the guitar of which I will

[1]See Murphy, R., p. 28.
[2]Abbatessa says three, but the context seems to contradict this.

describe only three principal ones: Firstly. Wanting to play a pattern such as this for example: B ⌐⌐⌐, you let the two fingers, middle and index, brush softly [downwards] and follow with the thumb, making the sound of the stroke [T] in three consecutive blows in the same amount of time as the stroke. For the upstroke you should do the opposite; the thumb begins up, followed by the index and middle.

The second way: having played the above, then make quickly and simply with all four fingers [a, m, i, p] one stroke [T] and repeat the pattern as above. You should use this style in slow pieces such as *Toccate, passi e mezi, Arie di Firenze* etc.

The third way will be, in playing this, for example C ⌐⌐⌐, you should brush downward with the middle finger, the thumb following and the index quickly makes the same motion, upwards and downwards making the strings sound many times repeated, adding with the index and middle fingers, i.e. so that the index will brush the strings in downward motion and the middle finger goes up. This method will pleasantly sort itself out by ear.   (Foscarini, c.1630, f.4-4ᵛ)

Foscarini is not terribly clear in his descriptions, but 'the first way' seems to require a triplet for each printed stroke, 'the second way' requires four notes per stroke, and 'the third way' appears to be a description of a continuous roll, such as might be used by Flamenco guitarists today.

Corbetta, in his 1671 book, provides us with an even more complicated version of the *repicco*:

Ex. 34

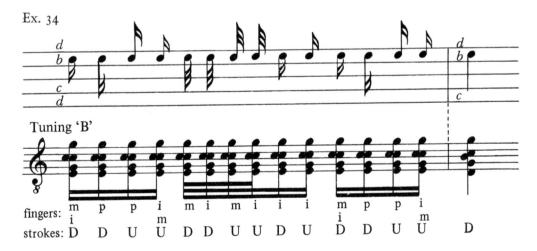

You will see the example of a *repicco* in a *Ciaccona* where the note with
the extended stem is played with the thumb. Having begun first with
the fingers, the thumb then plays the same and this is repeated as up-
beats. Notice that the four tied beats indicate that one must play the
first note with the middle finger, and the next with the index, and so
again as up strokes, all at a faster speed, and then continue with the
fingers and thumb [pattern]. (Ex. 34)

Ex. 35

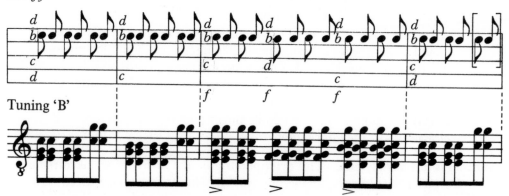

In the next *Ciaccona* you will see another *repicco*. . . . Where you see six
quaver strokes play four of them from the third course downwards,
and moving the hand, play the next two strokes on the other two
courses, the first and second, without touching the other [third, fourth,
and fifth] ones. After changing the chord, play in the same way for the
other six [quavers]. And changing the chord at the next four, hit the
first quaver loudly, and the other three softly. Do the same on changing
the chords at the other [groups of four] until the [pattern of the] first six
begins again. Where you find an *f* this means play the first of the four
strokes loudly, and in this way you will achieve a beautiful *repicco*.
(Ex. 35)   (Corbetta, 1671, p.3)

   As Sylvia Murphy has stated in her pioneering article on the subject, the *trillo* and
repicco 'should be noted by any performer of seventeenth-century guitar music wishing
to do justice to this still obscure field'.[3]

[3]Murphy, R., p. 31.

PIZZICATO STYLE (PUNTEADO)

In seventeenth-century guitar tablature, the general term for an ornament applied to a single note is, in Italian, *tremolo*, in French, *agrémen*, and in Spanish, *habilidade* or *afecto*. Each of those terms is defined as a short melodic formula gracing a single note. In other words, a *tremolo* does not *necessarily* refer to a *specific* ornament; it is also a generic term, and when a *tremolo* sign appears under a particular note, it *can* mean that the player may, if he chooses, apply *some ornament* to that note, be it a trill, a mordent, an *appoggiatura*, whichever is appropriate to the particular musical passage.

The ornaments will be discussed in the following order:

1. Trill
2. Mordent
3. Appoggiatura
4. Slur[4]
5. Vibrato[4]
6. Arpeggio

1. TRILL (Italian: *trillo* or *tremolo*; Spanish: *trino* or *aleado*; French: *tremblement*)

Despite their frequent use of trills, the guitar composers of the seventeenth century rarely tell us exactly how to play them, nor, it seems, is there any agreement amongst them as to what sign to use to indicate that a trill is to be played.

> This is the sign for the *trillo* ⅄. . Where it is found on a line, one ought to trill [trillar] that string. . . .　　　(Bartolotti, 1640, f.2ᵛ)

> The letter t, above or below the course indicates the *trillo* which is played with the most convenient finger of the left hand for as long as appropriate to the note so marked.
> 　　　　　　　　(Anonymous, *Conserto Vago*, 1645, p.3)

> The sign T· means the *tremolo*, which is made with the little finger on the first course in the chords C and E [of the *alfabeto*]. In the B it is made with the same finger on the fourth course. In the F chord it is made with the third finger on the third course. In the I chord it is made on the second course with the same finger, etc.　　(Calvi, 1646, p.6)

[4]The modern guitarist may be surprised to learn that in early guitar tablatures, the slur and vibrato were considered ornaments, and not, as they are today, an integral part of guitar playing technique. I think this fact should be considered of vital importance to anyone involved in the interpretation and performance of early guitar music.

You will also find a small line with two little dots like this: **⁎⁏** called *trino* or *aleado*. The Italians mark it with a T and two little dots. It is executed with the left hand by placing a convenient finger at the fret so marked with a number. Strike the course with another finger of the same hand without stopping, one or two frets ahead, according to the propriety of the chord.   (Guerau, 1684, f.5ᵛ)

Fortunately, the eccentric English composer, Thomas Mace, is considerably more specific in his description of the playing of trills, or 'shakes', as he calls them, in the French manner on the lute.

The shake, is 2 ways to be performed, either hard, or soft, the hard (or tearing-shake) is thus done, *viz.* If you shake any string open, you must first strike it with some right hand finger, and then be ready with the forefinger of the left hand to pick it up with the very tip (near the nail) of your finger; and so, by often, and quick picking it up in that manner, or (more plainly) scratching it, in a smooth, nimble, and strong agitation, you will have performed it.

The soft-shake, is done, in all respects, like the former, except the tearing, and the scratching; and only by beating the string strongly, and with a quick motion, in the same place, as you did the other; which always must be either in B, or C frett; and if it be done evenly, and strongly, it gives a very pleasant grace unto your play.

. . . I, for my own part, have had occasion to break both my arms; by reason of which, I cannot make the nerve-shake well, nor strong; yet, by a certain motion of my arm, I have gain'd such a contentive shake, that sometimes, my scholars will ask me, How they shall do to get the like? I have then no better answer for them, than to tell them, they must first break their arm, as I have done; and so possibly, after that, (by practice) they may get my manner of shake.

The stopt-shake, is (only) differing from the open-shake, in that you are always to use some one of your under-fingers, in your shaking, and to stop, one of your upper-fingers, upon some letter, and then shake with an under-finger. As for example, suppose you stop the letter B upon the 2nd string, with your fore-finger: Then must you make your shake, from the letter d, (because it is the aire) upon the same string, with your little finger; remembering to stop the B, hard and close, all the time of your shaking; and if you will have a soft, and smooth shake, then only beat the letter d hard, and quick, directly down, and up, with the very tip of your little finger; but if you would have a hard, or tearing shake, then nibble the d strongly, and very quick, and it will give you full content; and so for all stopt strings which require shaking. (Mace, 1676, p.103)

I cannot emphasize strongly enough the importance of reading the prefatory information given in each guitar book before coming to any decision regarding the meaning of ornament signs and how to play them. To illustrate, here is a table of the different signs used by guitar composers to indicate the trill.

T	Granata, 1674; Sanz (*trino*), 1674
T.[5]	Corbetta (*tremolo*), 1643; Calvi (*tremolo*), 1646; Granata (*tremolo*), 1646; Pellegrini (*tremolo*), 1650
.T.[5]	Foscarini (*tremolo*), c.1630
t	*Conserto Vago* (*trillo*), 1645; Corrette (*tremblement*), 1763
⁒	Bartolotti (*trillo*), 1640; Corbetta (*tremolo*), 1648; Guerau (*trino or aleado*), 1684
•	Valdambrini (*trillo*), 1648
)	De Visée (*tremblement*), 1682
x	Corbetta (*tremolo/tremblement*), 1671 and (*tremblement*) 1674; Campion (*tremblement*), 1705

You will note that Granata gives two different signs in two of his books, while Corbetta changes his use of both sign and term in almost every book he published! Clearly, the prefatory material of a specific guitar book can only be applied to the music therein, and one simply cannot assume that the same information will apply to the music found in another guitar book – even if both books were written by the same composer!

Trills can be played in a variety of ways:

Ex. 36

a. Main note trill (emphasis on written note)

---

[5] T· or ·T· could possibly mean one or two frets, respectively, are involved, i.e. a half or a whole step of the scale.

(Sixteenth Century)

b. Upper note trill (emphasis on auxiliary note)

In general, the main note trills are characteristic of much sixteenth-century string music and early seventeenth-century Italian guitar music. A useful source, contemporary with the earliest Spanish and French guitar music, is Tomás de Sancta Maria's *Libro llamodo Arte de tañer Fantasia assi para tecla como para vihuela* (1556). Although Sancta Maria's main purpose in the book is to explain music for keyboard instruments, he also, as his title page indicates, offers useful information for the *vihuela* and by implication the guitar, on both the short and the long main note trills.[6]

Robert Strizich, in his excellent article on Spanish ornamentation for the guitar, has come to the conclusion that the main note trill predominated throughout the seventeenth century in Spain.[7]

The upper note trill (with a turn), is found primarily at strong cadences in sixteenth- and early seventeenth-century music. By the mid-seventeenth century, French guitarists showed a marked preference for it, not only at cadences, but throughout the piece. By the mid-eighteenth century, rarely is any but the upper note trill called for. Here, for instance, is the only trill (*tremblement*) described by Corrette in his tutor of 1763:

Ex. 37

Cadence ou tremblement

Perhaps it would not be too broad a generalization to say that the main note trills, short or long, can be associated with earlier styles of music, and the upper note trills with later styles.

2. MORDENT (Italian: *mordente*; Spanish: *mordente*; French: *martellement, pincé*)

Fortunately, there is far less confusion surrounding the use of the mordent in early guitar tablatures; however, like the trill, signs for it do vary from source to source.

[6] See Poulton, H., p. 27.
[7] Strizich, O.

3. APPOGGIATURA (Italian: *appoggiatura, per appogiar le corde;* Spanish: *apoyamento, esmorsata, ligadura;* French: *cheute, petite chutte*)

There are two types of *appoggiatura,* the ascending and the descending, and various signs are used to indicate when to play them:

Descending:	T	Pesori, c.1650
	dx	Corbetta (*tremolo* or *tremblement*), 1671
	‿	Sanz (*esmorsata*), 1674

Ascending:	d‿	Bartolotti (*per appogiar le corde*), c.1655; Campion (*petite chutte*), 1705
	d⌒	Corbetta (*cheute*), 1671
	b‿	De Visée (*cheute*), 1682
	‿	Sanz (*apoyamento*), 1674

You will note that Sanz uses the same sign for the *appoggiatura* as he does for the mordent, and the same sign for both the descending and ascending *appoggiatura*. This is explained to a certain extent in his preface.

The *appoggiatura* is a frequently used ornament and is performed as follows:

Ex. 42

descending   ascending

The descending *appoggiatura* is found, contemporary with the first guitar books, in Milano's and Bŏrrono's *Intavolatura di lauto* of 1548. One of the rare instances of ornament indications in the printed music itself, it illustrates clearly what the composers intended, while a written explanation is also given in the preface. Diana Poulton translates it thus:

> . . . two fingers must be placed on the string and the finger on the lesser number must be held firm. Pull down the string with the finger which is on the higher number as if the voice were notated on the lesser of the two frets. This is done because the lute will sound sweeter.[8]

[8]Poulton, G., pp. 108-9.

Ex. 43

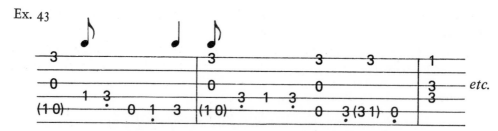

Later lute sources, such as Vallet in 1615 and Mersenne in 1636, continue to explain how to play *appoggiaturas*, and, by about 1650, we begin to find the descending type being written into the tablatures in a way remarkably similar to that of the 1548 source, with a little **T** (so we can be certain of the meaning of at least one guitarist's *tremolo*):

Ex. 44

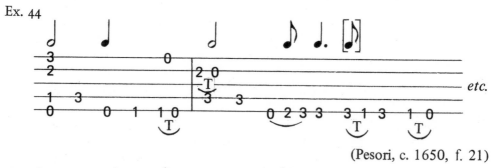

(Pesori, c. 1650, f. 21)

Bartolotti notates the ascending *appoggiatura* in this way:

Ex. 45

Corbetta gives us both types, the ascending, which he calls 'cheute', and the descending, which, like the trill in certain of his books, he calls 'tremolo' or 'tremblement':

Ex. 46   Cheutes

(Corbetta, 1671, p.9)

94

Gaspar Sanz has a specific Spanish name for each *appoggiatura: esmorsata* for the descending and *apoyamento* for the ascending.[9]

Thomas Mace, always an invaluable source of information on just about any topic you can name, tells us in more detail how they are done. He calls the descending *appoggiatura* the 'back-fall', and the ascending the 'half-fall', both of which are a lot less dangerous to perform than they sound.

> A back-fall, is only thus; viz. Let your note be what it will; It must first partake of the tone of another note, or half-note [i.e. whole or half step of the scale] above it, before it sound, as for example.
>
> Suppose I would back-fall "a," upon the treble string, then I must first stop "c," upon the same string, and strike it, as if it did absolutely intend "c" (only) should sound; yet so soon as I have so struck "c," I must, with the stopping finger (only) cause the "a" to sound, by taking it off, in a kind of twitch, so that the letter "a," may sound (by reason of that twitch, or falling back) presently after the letter "c," is struck, etc.
>
> This is called a back-fall, and there needs no more be said of it, (it being so easie to understand) . . .
>
> The half-fall, is ever from a half note [i.e. half step] beneath, (as is the beate) and is performed, by striking that half note first; but so soon, as that is so struck, you must readily clap down the true note, (with the proper finger, standing ready) without any further striking. Explained thus.
>
> Suppose I would make a half-fall to "f," upon the treble, (or any other string) I must place a finger in "e" upon the same string, and absolutely strike "e," as if nothing else were intended; but so soon as "e" has given its perfect sound, my next finger must fall smartly into "f"; so that "f" may sound strongly, only by that fall; which will cause a pritty, neat, and soft sound, without any other striking, and this is the half-fall. (Mace, 1676, pp.104-5)

Once again, Mace's instructions for playing ornaments on the lute tell us a great deal.

[9] See Strizich, O., p. 32.

4. SLUR (Italian: *strascino*; Spanish: *extrasino*; French: *tirade, cheute*)

Slurs, done with the left hand after plucking only the initial note with the right, are performed exactly as the guitarist is taught today, and are notated with curved lines above or below the tablature notes, thus:

Ex. 47

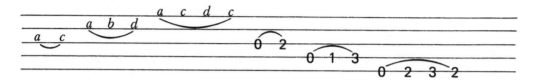

Because the sound of slurred notes is so different from that of the individually plucked ones, it is not surprising that the early guitarists and lutenists considered them to be separate ornamental devices. In the tablatures, slurs are used in groups of from two to six notes, and are normally placed according to string changes (see above).

Occasionally, one finds a large slur mark which takes in more than one course on the guitar. I can only surmise that the intention here is for the player himself to divide the slur into more than one, according to the string change principle:

Ex. 48

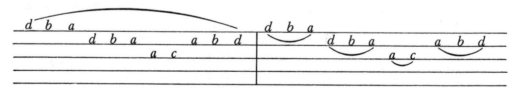

It should be noted that slurs are absent from sixteenth-century tablatures, be they lute or guitar, printed books or manuscripts. As far as I know, the first appearance of slur marks is in Girolamo Kapsperger's *Libro primo d'intavolatura di chitarrone* (1604). Its first appearance in a guitar source seems to be in Foscarini's book of c.1630. I think it would be reasonable to assert, therefore, that slurs should not be used in the earlier guitar repertoire. Just the opposite applies, however, to guitar music of the seventeenth century, in which slurs were used to produce some quite interesting rhythmic effects. Here, groupings of slurs tend to be quite irregular, often going over the bar lines. The first note of a slur group is naturally stronger than the rest (being the only one plucked), and this produces rhythmic stresses in all parts of the bar. For example:

(*Chiacona* – Corbetta, 1648, p.29)

This rhythmic variety is important in all the guitar music of this period, and for that reason, one should not be tempted to iron out and regularize the slur patterns, as has been done in so many modern transcriptions of this music. To do so is to completely disregard the composer's intentions. At the risk of being accused of repeating myself, might I once again remind the guitarist that he can only be true to the music if he learns to read the original tablatures.

5. VIBRATO (Italian: *acento, accento; trillo, tremolo sforzato*; Spanish: *temblor*; French: *miolement, plainte, flatement*)

The signs for vibrato are:

Foscarini, c.1630; Bartolotti, 1640 (*trillo sforzato*); Corbetta, 1643 and 1648 (*tremolo sforzato*); Corbetta, 1671 (*acento* or *flatement*); Sanz, 1674 (*temblor*); De Visée, 1682 (*miolement*); Guerau, 1694 (*temblor*); Campion, 1705 (*miaulement*); Corrette, 1763 (*plainte*)

Pellegrini, 1650 (*tremolo sforzato*)

Vibrato was used primarily on higher pitched notes; only occasionally was it found in the bass. As the Italian name, *accento*, implies, it was used to accent and emphasize specific notes, usually the highest one in a phrase.

Vibrato is described as suitable for the *vihuela* as early as 1557 by Luis Venegas de Henestrosa in his *Libro de cifra nueva para tecla, harpa y vihuela*.[10] Lute writers describe it from the early seventeenth century onwards. Foscarini is the first to describe its use for the guitar:

[10]See Poulton, G., p. 109.

> A sharp sign being placed under a number: ✕ . . . , you should
> separate the [thumb of the left] hand from the guitar, putting the most
> convenient finger at the number shown, and shake the hand back and
> forth. This will produce, as far as possible, a sustaining, bit by bit, of the
> sound of the string. . . .   (Foscarini, c.1630, f.3)

You will notice that he tells us to free the left hand from the neck. This point is also
made by several other guitar writers, and implies a very strong vibrato. Still other
writers, however, do not mention the freeing of the hand at all:

> This sign: ✕ like a double *tremolo* is called *Acento*. It is made by
> shaking the [left] hand with the finger fixed on the note of the course
> to which [the sign] is put.   (Corbetta, 1671, p.3)

> This sign: ✕ indicates *temblor*. It is performed by plucking the string
> with the right hand and then moving the left hand from side to side
> without lifting the finger from the fret.   (Guerau, 1694, f.4ᵛ)

6. ARPEGGIO (Italian: *arpeggio*; Spanish: *harpeado*; French: *arpège*)

The signs for the *arpeggio* are:

⁒⁒ *Conserto Vago*, 1645; Valdambrini, 1648; Bartolotti, c.1655; Sanz, 1674

⁒⁒ Roncalli, 1692

ℐℐ Pellegrini, 1650; Matteis, 1682

Arpeggiated chords belong more to the seventeenth and eighteenth centuries than
to the sixteenth, and naturally so, since the main style of lute and guitar music, with
the notable and important exception of the *battente* style, was contrapuntal until the
early seventeenth century. By this time, chords of long duration were often orna-
mented in this fashion by breaking them up into individual notes, sometimes quite
elaborately.

The first mention of the *arpeggio* for the guitar came in 1601, when Scipione Cerreto
talked about it in relation to the four-course guitar:

> And when such an instrument is played *arpiggiando* with all of the
> fingers of the right hand, it makes a beautiful effect. But this method of
> playing should be learned with long practice.   (Cerreto, 1601, p.321)

In the preface to the anonymous *Conserto Vago* (1645), the *arpeggio* sign ⁒ is
explained, but only used in the *tiorba* part, not in the *chitarrino* part.

The first clear-cut instruction for its use on the guitar is by Valdambrini, who, prior
to explaining how it is done, specifically mentions that he is following the fashion of

98

Girolamo Kapsperger:

> The sign for *arpegiare* is this ⁒ . It is made by touching the course separately, with the first note played with the thumb, the second note with the index, the highest note with the middle finger, and the other with the index. For example:

Ex. 50

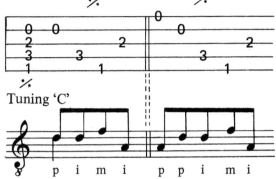

> . . . reiterating the pattern four times in order to last for the duration [of the note] written above.   (Valdambrini, 1648, p.2)

This, in fact, is an unusual pattern for arpeggiation, which clearly derives from the *chitarrone* (or theorbo), of which Kapsperger[11] was an important exponent. For the *chitarrone*, the first two courses are to be tuned an octave lower than the lute, the third course becomes the highest pitched, and, consequently, the one on which the melody line is most often played.[12] Given that Valdambrini tunes his guitar in the fashion recommended by Gaspar Sanz, with the lowest pitch being that of the third course, the last note in Valdambrini's example of the *arpeggio* ends at the bottom of the chord!

Other writers have given us the following patterns:

Ex. 51

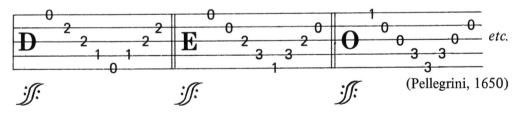

(Pellegrini, 1650)

[11]If copies of Kapsperger's two lost guitar books are ever found, they may shed more light on this unusual *chitarrone*-style *arpeggio*.

[12]See Spencer, C.

Ex. 51 (cont.)

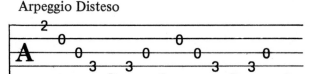

Arpeggio Disteso

(Bartolotti, c. 1655)

Gaspar Sanz discussed *arpeggios*, but did not actually notate any with the sign he gives. He does, however, have a *Preludio o capricho arpeado*, completely written out in arpeggio style.[13]

By and large, the implication from the guitar books is that ornamental *arpeggios*, where appropriate to a long-held chord, can be played at the discretion of the player, even when not specifically indicated by a sign.

For a comprehensive survey on early ornamentation, one should consult Robert Donington's *The Interpretation of Early Music*.[14] In it, Donington presents a wealth of information drawn from non-guitar sources, and including vocal, lute, viol, and keyboard ornamentation. A word of warning, however, to the guitarist: Do not study baroque keyboard ornamentation as a guide to that of the guitar. Each instrument has its own idioms and its own technical abilities (quite irrespective of the individual player's). The harpsichord, for example, allows the player to perform astonishingly intricate ornaments with ease, and has, as a result, developed its own traditions of ornamentation which often have very little bearing on those of other instruments. Because keyboard music has received such an enormous amount of attention and has been so much more available in modern editions, many guitarists have studied it and tried to apply some of its ornaments to baroque guitar music, not surprisingly, without too much success. In fact, if modern editions of baroque guitar music are not yet available to you, and you are not able to read the original guitar tablatures, it is far more sensible to go to the repertoire of the guitar's closest relative, the lute, for which there has been a growing body of modern editions in recent years.

---

[13]p. 11.
[14](London, 1974).

Ce qui eft deffous les lettres, c'eft pour tirer de la main droite, le point feul c'eft pour le premier doit, les 2, points font pour le deuxiéme doit, & le trait de deffous c'eft pour tirer du pouce.

Cette barre droite c'eft pour tirer enfemble.

Ces barres de travers font pour feparer.

Cheutes.

Tirades.

Tremblements.

Martellements.

Miolements ou Plaintes.

Pour coucher le premier doit.

Tenües

Points muets.

Plate 17
N. Derosier: *Les Principes de la guitarre* [1696], pp.ii and iii.

Plate 18
F. Corbetta: *La Guitarre Royalle* (1671), p.9.

8

THE GUITAR AS A CONTINUO INSTRUMENT

Perhaps the most important function of the guitar in all periods of its existence has been as a chordal instrument, accompanying the voice and playing in ensemble. The earliest guitar music presents the vocal accompaniment fully written out in tablature. Later accompaniments are supplied by the *alfabeto* system. But, from the seventeenth century, with the widespread use of a system whereby a semi-improvised accompaniment was devised from the bass part, the guitar joined the harpsichord, lute, theorbo, etc., as a continuo-playing instrument.[1] The system was sometimes called thorough-bass, *basso continuo*, or, playing *sopra la parte*, and required a knowledge of what sort of chord to play over various notes in the written bass line. Often a system of figures (numbers) was used as a musical shorthand to indicate in skeletal fashion what the harmonies should be; today we commonly call this practice 'playing from a figured bass'.

The style of accompaniments varied from strumming, particularly in dance music (in a fashion approaching modern 'rhythm guitar' playing), to plucking, using the same technique as for solo music. Corbetta includes a brief section on playing *sopra la partie* in his 1643 book, as does Foscarini in 1640 (*Quinto libro*). But, undoubtedly, the most comprehensive and the best guidance for guitar continuo comes to us from Nicola Matteis, whose book was written in Italy c.1680, and republished in England in 1682. Matteis teaches us what chords to play over the bass line, how to read figures, what to do at cadences, how to overcome the problems of rapid and difficult basses, styles of accompaniment, and he also adds a few solos for good measure! Here is the title page and preface, which show his intentions, and, in facsimile, a selection of charts and directions:

f.1   The False Consonances of Musick or instructions for the playing of a true base upon the guitarre, with choice examples and clear directions to enable any man in a short time to play all musical ayres. A great help likewise to those that would play exactly upon the harpsichord, lute or base-viol, shewing the delicacy of all accords and how to apply them in their proper places. In Foure parts by Nicola Matteis.

[1]This is not the place to set down the rules and system of continuo practice. For this see Donington, I., pp.288-372, and Arnold, A., and for particular reference to usage for plucked instruments, see the theorbo section of Thomas Mace's *Musick's Monument*, 1676, facsimile edition: Paris, 1966.

1ᵛ   The first part lays down rules & directions for playing on ye Thorough Bass with references to examples. The second part hath severall bases to work upon accommodated both to the making of the hand & enforming ye understanding. The third part treats of all such accords both ordinary & extraordinary as were not exemplified before. The fourth part sets forth ye Universall scale very usefull and easy for young beginners to lead them to all ye marks in musick distinctly either flatt or sharp. . . .

To the Reader

2   The guitarre was never so much in use & credit as it is at this day, & finding it emproved to so great a perfection, it is my present design to make it company for other instruments. Every body knows it to be an imperfect instrument & yet finding upon experience how agreeable a part it bears in a consort I have composed severall pieces both for ye practise & enformation of those that would make use of it with ye harpsecord, lute, theorbo, or base-viol. I might undertake for ye curiosity & usefullness of ye pieces which I have published to ye world in this book but I shall rather refer my self to ye ingenious peruser of it upon further consideration.

2ᵛ   It will not be amiss to advertise the reader in this one point further; that it was not possible to bring this book in to a narrower compass then now it is; so as to answer all ye purposes of the Author in the publication of it. By reason of ye necessity of so many instances upon every difficulty, without which, it would in many cases have been very obscure.   Nicola Matteis

The first Lesson which Schollars ought to learn by heart,

Plate 19
a) Page 8.

In case you find a cadence of a whole measure the way to hold your time out is by giving three stroakes upon the fowrth and after a shake upon a third as in the first example you may see,

And lickwise when you find a cadence of half a measure you shall doe as y second example sherveth and the rest as followes.

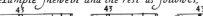

Many times you will find severall cadence that runs an Eight down as thus in such a case you must play just as if it was soe because the Guitarre has not such low eights upon any other key you must doe the same

b) Page 13.

Where you must strike the accords,

When you find the quavers in common time sett after this manner it will be sufficient to strike y full accords to y first of every two vid pag: 30.
But if the movement be very quick after this manner then stricke y full accords only to y first of every fourth vid pag: 31.
And the same to every foure of semiquavers vid pag: 39.
But if the movement be extraordinary swift as thus so that your hand cannot perform it then stricke y first note of every foure and let the other three alone it being only a division vid pag: 39.
1. If y movement in triple time be slow you must strick y accord to eatch crotchett. Fol. 44.
2. If it be quick then to the first of every three vid pag: 42.
3. If it be all quavers after this manner then to the first of every Six vid pag 43.

c) Page 19.

How many Strokes you ought to give to every note to keep true time.

In common time to a semibrief which is this note ☐ you must give a stroke downe of the time of a minum, & two strokes more ÿ one downe ÿ other up. Crochet time so ☐ which makes it trew time Fol. 36. example.

To a minum that is this note ☐ you may give two Strokes ÿ one down ÿ other up so ☐ Fol. 27. example and other sorts of notes you must observe ÿ examples in the first part of the Booke,

In triple time the prickt minum so ☐ you must give one Stroke downe worth two Crochets & an other up worth one Crochet so ☐ Fol. 28. example you may also play it in an other maner that is one Stroake down, and two up so ☐ as Fol. 45. will show you you must besure to owe ÿ two Stroakes up very sweet

And take notice in triple time somtimes the movement goes so fast that this sort of noat ☐ you are to give no more then one stroak so striking it very Quick. ☐

d) Page 20.

Esempio Fasile.

2

Quando il Scolaro principia ad'intendere le note all'ora puol esercitare qualche basso facile, è toccarlo, con buona maniera esempio

e) Page 27.

9

OTHER GUITARS AND RELATED INSTRUMENTS

BANDURRIA

A small plucked instrument derived from the guitar. Next to nothing is known about its physical appearance in the sixteenth century, but we do know, from Bermudo's discourse (*Libro Quarto*, cap. xcvii and xcviii) that it was a small, treble instrument with three strings (gut?), tuned in fifths (no pitches given). Sometimes the three strings were tuned to a fourth and a fifth, or vice versa. According to Bermudo, players may have developed the *bandurria* by shortening the guitar and reducing the number of strings. Some players used no frets, some used six or seven, but the instrument was difficult to fret because of its short string length. He goes on to say that a fourth string could be added, and that he had seen five-string *bandurrias* from America. In the seventeenth and eighteenth centuries, the *bandurria* acquired five and six double courses, and was mostly played (with a plectrum) as the treble in an ensemble. And this is precisely how the *bandurria* is still played today. A brief tutor for the later, five-course *bandurria* (tuned c^{I}♯c^{I}♯, f^{I}♯f^{I}♯, b^{I}b^{I}, e^{II}e^{II}, a^{II}a^{II}) is Pablo Minguet y Yrol's *Reglas . . . para tañer la bandurria . . .* c.1752? (This is part of a series by Minguet and is usually bound with the booklets for guitar and other instruments.)

CHITARRIGLIA

A small five-course guitar, tuned like the Spanish guitar, but at a higher pitch (e.g. first course at g^{I} or a^{I}). Several seventeenth-century guitar books mention this instrument, including those by Calvi, Granata, and Pesori. The so-called 'Ausseer Gitarre-tabulatur,' a manuscript found in Vienna (Nationalbibliothek, MS. S.m.9659) shows in staff notation and tablature the following tuning: cc^{I}, ff^{I}, b♭[b♭], d^{I} [d^{I}], g^{I} and a similar one a tone lower. The small guitar by Diaz, described in the chapter on THE FIVE-COURSE GUITAR, is probably a *chitarriglia*.

CHITARRINO

The Italian name for the small four-course guitar. It was sometimes also known as *chitarra Italiana* and *chitarra da sette corde*.

CHITARRA BATTENTE

A five-course guitar of varying size, which was designed for wire strings of brass and low-tempered steel. The strings were not always arranged in pairs; sometimes, as later examples show, they were arranged in groups of three. The instrument had a thin, movable bridge, held in place by the pressure of the strings stretching over it to the lower end of the body, and had a bend in the soundboard, starting below the bridge, which counteracted the downward pressure of the strings. This feature is similar on the Neapolitan mandolin. Unlike any other members of the guitar family, the *chitarra battente* had inlaid bone or metal frets to accommodate the wire strings. Its back was usually vaulted, like many ordinary guitars of the time, but its sides tended to be rather steep. It was played with a quill plectrum and was probably confined to the performance of *alfabeto* music. The term *chitarra battente* seems to be a recent one, originating in the nineteenth and early twentieth centuries, when it was still in use in remote regions of Italy. The main evidence of construction and ornament styles on the surviving instruments, and parallel developments on the Neapolitan mandolin, suggest that this kind of guitar first appeared in the mid-eighteenth century. Supposed early examples, such as the 1624 Jacob Stadler guitar (London, W. E. Hill & Sons, see Baines, E., No. 291) could easily have originally been normal guitars which were converted at a later date. (This has been the fate of countless existing museum specimens.) No specific music for the *chitarra battente* has survived, and this fact, coupled with the rough construction of most of the authentic *chitarre battenti* in collections, could mean that it was mostly a folk or popular guitar, not used for art music.

ENGLISH GUITAR

This instrument is vastly different from the gut-strung guitar, and was actually a revival of the cittern. Although not the kind of instrument I have been concerned with in this book, a brief discussion of it is necessary due to the large amount of music for it from the mid-eighteenth century, the title pages of which all say, either for 'guitar' or 'guittar'. Hence, unless one is able to distinguish which music is for the 'English' guitar and which is for the Spanish guitar, much confusion can result.

The English guitar was known in France as the *cistre* or *guittare allemande* (indicating its German origin),[1] and in Italy as the *cetra*. Italian musicians apparently introduced and started the fashion for the instrument in England. The earliest music for it in England is Pasqualini de Marzi's *Six sonatas for the cetra or Kitara* . . . (c.1740; copy in London,

---

[1]The revival of these instruments seems to begin with the five-course, so called 'bell-cittern', made in Hamburg (also known as the *cithrinchen*). A six-course chordal tuning for an instrument called a 'guitarre' is in J. F. B. Majer's *Neueroffneter Theoretischer und Praktischer Musick Saal* . . . Nuremberg (1741). This tuning is similar to that of other wire-strung 'guitarres'.

British Library). It soon, however, became known simply as the 'guittar'.

The standard tuning for the instrument was to a C major chord, beginning with C below middle C: c, e, gg, c¹c¹, e¹e¹, g¹g¹. The strings were of brass and steel and were played with the right-hand fingers. At first, tablature was used, but this soon gave way to staff notation, entirely in the treble clef. The music relied upon the use of many open strings, and the use of parallel thirds, which were easy to play with this tuning. Hence, the things to look for in order to distinguish English guitar music from Spanish guitar music are: the predominant use of the key of C; much use of parallel thirds; the lowest notes as middle C on the staff[2] (the instrument sounds an octave lower than written); and the typical configurations of chords, such as:

Ex. 52

Representative publications for the English guitar include: Anonymous, *Ladies Pocket Guide or the compleat tutor for the guittar* . . . (c.1750); G. Rush, *Favourite lessons or airs for 2 guittars* . . . (c.1755); Anonymous, *The compleat Tutor for guittar* . . . (c.1755); R. Bremner, *Instructions for the guitar* . . . (1758); J. F. Zuchert, *Six sonatas or solos for the guitar and bass* . . . (1759); F. Geminiani, *The art of playing the guitar or cittra* . . . (1760); R. Straube, *Lessons for two guittars* . . . (c.1765), and *Three Sonatas for the guitar* . . . (1768); J. C. Bach, *A sonata for the guitar* . . . (c.1775).

Music for the instrument continued to be published until the early nineteenth century.

MANDOLA

The term normally refers to the mandolin, or a larger, tenor-sized mandolin, which is a gut-strung, plectrum-played instrument that has been used for centuries. But Bonanni's *Gabinetto Armonico* . . . (1716), illustrates the mandola as a tiny, four-course guitar the size of a modern ukulele (see Plate 20). See also the Spanish term, VANDOLA.

THEORBOED GUITAR (*chitarra tiorbata*)

A guitar with an extension attached to the side of its normal peghead for longer, extra bass strings. These basses were played as open, unfingered strings, and supple-

---

[1]One occasionally encounters music for a seven-course instrument with a low G string.

LIII   *Mandola.*

Plate 20
Bonanni: *Gabinetto Armonico* (1716), plate LIII.

110

mented the normal stopped strings on the fingerboard. This principle of adding an extension was known on lutes from the late sixteenth century.[3] For the guitar, the earliest such arrangement is mentioned in 1640 by G. B. Doni in his *Annotazioni . . . pp.355-7*. The instrument he proposes is a highly novel one, having an arrangement of three separate necks (!) on one body to accommodate the three theoretical tuning systems he advocates. It is unlikely that anyone ever built this instrument. The extended necks, going beyond the first pegheads, each carry four extra basses to what appear to be only four courses of fingered strings (see Plate 21). The theorboed guitar seems to have been in use, as there is music for it in Granata's 1659 book[4] and in the De Gallot manuscript (Oxford, Bodleian Mus. sch. C94). Antonio Stradivari has left his measurements for the peghead and extension of a 'citara tiorbata' with five double courses on the first peghead and seven single basses on the second,[5] but the spelling of the name suggests that the instrument is actually a cittern.[6] There is a surviving example, made in France, of a theorboed guitar from c.1770, but this has been converted to a single-strung instrument.[7]

TIPLE

The Spanish term for the treble guitar. Minguet y Yrol gives the five courses tuned as: f¹¹f¹¹, bb, d¹d¹, g¹g¹, c¹¹c¹¹ (notice the unusual interval arrangement), and De Sotos gives them as: ee, aa, d¹d¹, f¹♯f¹♯, b¹b¹. (See also CHITARRIGLIA.)

VANDOLA

The Spanish term for the five- or six-course mandola or mandolin. It is discussed in the guitar books of Amat, Minguet y Yrol (Plate 22), and De Sotos. The tuning given by all three is: dd, gg, c¹c¹, e¹e¹, a¹a¹, d¹¹d¹¹, one of the common interval arrangements of the mandola of the time.

---

[3]See Spencer, C.

[4]Granata gives a *Preludio*, two *correntes*, a *saraband*, and a *Capriccio* for the '*chitarra Atiorbata*'. The instrument requires twelve courses, i.e. seven additional unstopped basses to the five courses on the fingerboard.

[5]Illustrated in Sacconi, S., p.227.

[6]For instance, the anonymous *Secondo libro d'intavolatura di citara* . . . (1602), is often cited in guitar bibliographies, but it is, in fact, for a six-course cittern. See Tyler, C.

[7]Illustrated in Thibault, E., p.94.

Plate 21
G. B. Doni: *Annotazioni* (1640), plate 356.

112

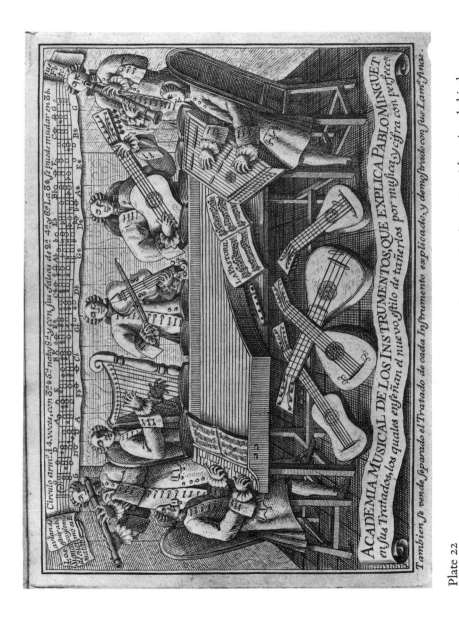

Plate 22

Frontispiece to Minguet y Yrol: *Reglas* (c.1752), showing the large Spanish guitar behind the harpsichord and in front, from left to right: tiple, vandola, citara, bandurria. The citara (cittern) uses metal strings and a plectrum. The plectrum is shown on both the citara and the bandurria.

Plate 23
Fantasie by Adrian le Roy (*Premier livre*, 1551), f.3ᵛ-4.

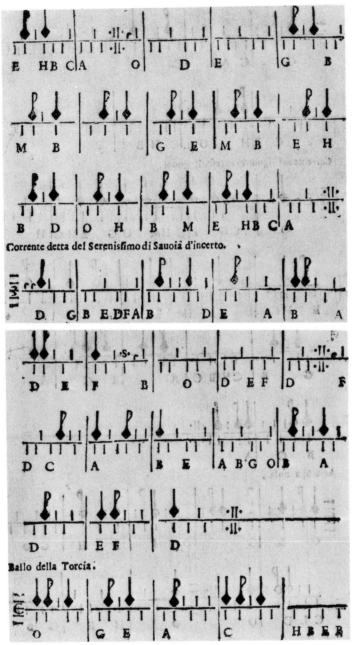

Plate 24
Corrente from Benedetto Sanseverino (*Intavolatura facile*, 1620), pp.68–69.

Plate 25
Three fantasies by Miguel de Fuenllana (*Libro de musica*, 1554), ff.164ᵛ-165.

Fantasias – Fuenllana (*continued*).

Plate 26
Toccata by G. B. Granata (*Novi capricci armonici*, 1674), pp.30-31.

Alemanda

Toccata – Granata (*continued*).

Plate 27
Toccata by F. Corbetta (*Varii capricii*, 1643), p.7.

Plate 28
Pavanas, Jiga and Bailete frances by Gaspar Sanz (*Instruccion*, 1674), f.47.

Plate 29
Sarabande la stuarde by F. Corbetta (*La Guitarre royalle* 1671), f.71

APPENDIX I

PRIMARY SOURCES

This list comprises printed books and manuscripts containing music for solo guitar to c.1800. Various important treatises containing information on the guitar are also included. The list is drawn from the various volumes of RISM (*Répertoire International des Sources Musicales*, 1960–   ), available to date, and the locations of sources follow the standard RISM sigla. For example: GB:Lbm = Great Britain:London, British Museum. The sigla are explained at the beginning of each RISM volume and in Brown, I. The list also incorporates those of Wolf, H., Danner, B., Danner, U., and Kirkendale, A. The printed books are listed in chronological order and the earliest ones are fully described in Brown, I. His numbering system is quoted for these (e.g. 1546_{14}). Items in square brackets are volumes which no longer exist. Beside each entry is my code for tuning types (A, B, or C) and other information. The code is as follows:

    X = four-course guitar (five-course guitar is otherwise meant unless noted to the contrary)

    I = plain Italian tablature

    F = French tablature with or without stroke signs

    O = Alfabeto only (or Spanish chord tablature)

    M = Mixed Italian tablature

    S = Staff notation

I have applied these code letters only where I am reasonably sure they apply.

I. PRINTED SOURCES

DATE	AUTHOR AND TITLE	TUNING	REMARKS
1546_{14}	MUDARRA, Alonso, *Tres libros de Musica* . . . E:E, E:Mm, CH:Zz		X, I, mostly *vihuela*
1549_2	BARBERIIS, Melchiore de, *Opera Intitolata Contina* . . . A:Wn, D-brd:W, F:Pthibault, GB:Lbm		X, I (top line = 1st course), mostly lute
$[1550]_2$	MORLAYE, Guillaume, *Tablature de guiterne* . . .		
1551_1	GORLIER, Simon, *Le Troysieme Livre* . . . *De Guiterne* . . . CH:SGv		X, F

1551₃	Le Roy, Adrian, *Premier Livre de Tablature de Guiterre . . .* F:Pm, GB:Lbm	X, F
[1551]₄	Le Roy, Adrian, *Briefve et facile instruction pour apprendre la tablature a bien accorder, conduire et disposer la main sur la guiterne*	
1552₃	Le Roy, Adrian, *Tiers Livre . . . De Guiterre . . .* F:Pm, GB:Lbm	X, F
1552₅	Morlaye, Guillaume, *Le Premier Livre . . . De Guiterne . . .* CH:SGv	X, F
1552₆	Morlaye, Guillaume, *Quatriesme Livre . . . De Guyterne & . . . De la Cistre . . .* CH:SGv	X, F
1553₃	Brayssing, Gregoire, *Quart Livre . . . De Guiterre . . .* F:Pm, GB:Lbm	X, F
1553₄	Morlaye, Guillaume, *Le Second Livre . . . De Guiterne . . .* CH:SGv	X, F
1554₃	Fuenllana, Miguel de, *Libro de Musica Para Vihuela . . .* A:Iu, A:Wn, E:Bc, E:E, E:Mn (4 copies), F:Pc, F:Pn, GB:Lbm, US:Cn, US:NYp, US:Wc	X and 5 course, I, mostly *vihuela*
1554₄	Le Roy, Adrian, *Cinquiesme Livre de Guiterre . . .* F:Pm, GB:Lbm	X, F
1556₈	Le Roy, Adrian, *Second Livre de Guiterre . . .* F:Pm, GB:Lbm	X, F
[1568]₉	Rowbotham, James (ed.), *The breffe and playne instruction to lerne to play on the gyttron and also the cetterne*	
[156?]₂	Gorlier, Simon, *Livre de Tablature de Guiterne*	
1570₄	Phalèse, P. and Bellère, J. (eds.), *Selectissima in Guiterna Ludenda Carmina . . .* D-ddr:ROu (2 copies)	X, F
[1573]₇	Phalèse, P. and Bellère, J. (eds.), *Selectissima carmina ludenda in Quinterna . . .*	
[1578]₇	Le Roy, Adrian, *Briefve & facile instruction . . . sur la Guiterne*	
[1586]₁	Amat, Juan Carlos, *Guitarra Española . . .*	Treatise
[158?]₃	Giuliani, Girolamo, *Intavolatura de Chitara . . .*	
[1596]	Amat, Juan Carlos, *Guitarra Española . . .*	

1601	CERRETO, Scipione, *Della prattica musicale* . . . Naples B:Br, Dbrd:B, F:B, F:Pc, F:Pn, GB:Lbm (2 copies), I:Bc, I:Fm, I:Nc, I:Nn, I:Rsc, US:AA, US:Cn, US:Wc		X, I, treatise
1606	MONTESARDO, Girolamo, *Nuova inventione d'intavolatura per sonare li balletti sopra la chitarra spagnuola* . . . Florence A:Wgm, I:Bc	A	O
1608	PICO, Foriano, *Nuova scelta di sonate per la chitarra spagnola* . . . Naples I:Nn	A	O
1609	PICO, Foriano, *Nuova scelta di sonate per la chitarra spagnola* . . . Rome F:Pn	A	O
1618	ANONYMOUS, *Il Primo libro d'intavolatura della chitarra spagnuola* . . . Rome I:Rsc	A	O
1620	COLONNA, Giovanni Ambrosio, *Intavolatura di chitarra alla spagnuola* . . . Milan GB:Lbm, I:Bc	A	O
1620	COLONNA, Giovanni Ambrosio, *Il secundo libro d'intavolatura di chittarra alla spagnuola* . . . Milan I:Ma	A	O
1620	SANSEVERINO, Benedetto, *Intavolatura facile* . . . *per la chitarra alla spagnuola* . . . *opera terza* . . . Milan GB:Lbm	A	O
[1622]	MILANUZZI, Carlo, *Secondo scherzo delle ariose* . . .		
1622	SANSEVERINO, Benedetto, *Il primo libro d'intavolatura per la chitarra alla spagnuola* . . . *opera terza (ristampato)* Milan I:Bc	A	O
1623	COLONNA, Giovanni Ambrosio, *Il terzo libro d'intavolatura di chitarra alla spagnuola* . . . Milan I:Bc	A	O
1623	MILANUZZI, Carlo, *Terzo scherzo delle ariose* . . . *opera nona* . . . Venice D-brd:Hs, I: Mc	A	O
1624	ARANIES, Juan, *Libro Segundo de tonos y villancicos a una dos tres y quatro voces, con la zifra de la guitarra espannola a la usanza Romana,* Rome I:Bc	A	O
[1624]	MILLIONI, Pietro, *Il primo, secondo, et terzo libro d'intavolatura* . . .		
c.1625	ANONYMOUS, *Il vero modo per imparare sonare le chitarriglia spagnuola* . . . Perugia source	A	O

unknown

1625	MILANUZZI, Carlo, *Secondo scherzo delle ariose vaghezze . . . opera ottava (ristampa)* Venice (=[1622]) I:Bc	A	O
1626	AMAT, Juan Carlos, *Guitarra Española de cinco ordenes, la qual enseña de templar, y tañer rasgado . . .* Lérida US:Cn	A	O, treatise
1626	BRIÇEÑO, Luis de, *Metodo mui facilissimo para aprender a tañer la guitarra a lo español . . .* Paris F:Pn	C	O
1627	ABBATESSA, Giovanni Battista, *Corona di vaghi fiori . . .* Venice GB:Lbm	A	O
1627	AMAT, Juan Carlos, *Guitarra española de cinco ordenes, la qual enseña de templar, y tañer rasgado . . .* Lérida E:Mn	A	O, treatise
1627	COLONNA, Giovanni Ambrosio, *Intavolatura di chitarra spagnuola del primo, secondo, terzo, quarto libro . . .* Milan I:Nn	A	O
1627	COSTANZO, Fabrizio, *Fior novello Libro I . . .* Bologna I:Bc	A	O
1627	MILLIONI, Pietro, *Quarta impressione del primo, secondo, et terzo libro d'intavolatura . . .* Rome, G. Facciotti I:Bc	A	O
1627	MILLIONI, Pietro, *Seconda impressione del Quarto Libro d'intavolatura di Chitarra Spagnola . . .* Rome, G. Facciotti GB:Lbm	A	O
1627	MILLIONI, Pietro, *Prima impressione del Quinto Libro d'intavolatura di Chitarra Spagnola . . .* Rome, G. Facciotti I:Bc	A	O
1627	MILLIONI, Pietro, *Corona del primo, secondo e terzo libro d'intavolatura di chitarra spagnola . . .* Rome I:Bc	A	O, and O for X
c.1627	MILLIONI, Pietro and MONTE, Lodovico, *Vero e facil modo d'imparare . . . la Chitarra spagnola . . .* Venice, A. Salvadori NL:DHgm	A	O
1629	FOSCARINI, Giovanni Paolo, *Intavolatura di chitarra spagnola . . . libro secondo . . .* Macerata F:LM	B	O

c.1630	FOSCARINI, Giovanni Paolo, *Il primo, secondo, e terzo libro della chitarra spagnola* D-ddr:Bds, I:Bc	B	M
1631	MILLIONI, Pietro, *Corona del primo, secondo, e terzo libro* . . . Milan (=1627) F:Pthibault	A	O, and O for X
1631	MILLIONI, Pietro, *Corona del primo, secondo, e terzo libro* . . . *Nuovamente stampata* . . . Rome US:Wc	A	O, and O for X
c.1632	FOSCARINI, Giovanni Paolo, *I quatro libri della chitarra spagnola* . . . F:Pn, E:Mn, GB:Cu, GB:Lbm, GB:London, R. Spencer's private library	B	M
1635	ABBATESSA, Giovanni Battista, *Cespuglio di varii fiori* . . . Orvieto GB:Lbm	A	O
1635	MILLIONI, Pietro, *Quarta impressione del primo, seconda, et terzo libro* . . . Turin (=1627) I:Bc	A	O
1636	MERSENNE, Marin, *Harmonie universelle* . . . Paris Many copies including: B:Br, F:Pn, GB:Lbm, US:Cn, US:Wc	C	F, treatise
1636	MONTE, Lodovico, *Vago fior di virtu* . . . *la chitarriglia spagnuola* . . . Venice I:Bc	A	O
1637	ABBATESSA, Giovanni Battista, *Cespuglio di varii fiori* . . . Florence (=1635) F:Pthibault, I:Bc	A	O
1637	COLONNA, Giovanni Ambrosio, *Intavolatura di chitarra spagnuola del primo, secondo, terzo, quatro libro* . . . *Nuovamente Ristampata* Milan ([=1627]) GB:Lbm, I:Bc	A	O
1637	MILLIONI AND MONTE, *Vero e facil modo* . . . *la Chitarra spagnola* . . . Rome & Macerata, S. & A. Grisei (=c.1627) GB:Lbm	A	O
1637	SFONDRINO, Giovanni Battista, *Trattenimento virtuoso* . . . *sonate per la chitarra* . . . Milan source unknown		
1639	AMAT, Juan Carlos, *Guitarra española* . . . Gerona E:Mn	A	O
1639	CORBETTA, Francesco, *De gli scherzi armonici* . . . Bologna I:Bc, I:Nc	B	O, M
1639	TROMBETTI, Agostino, *Intavolatura di sonate* . . . *libro primo e due* . . . I:Bc	A	O

1640	BARTOLOTTI, Angiolo Michele, *Libro primo di chitarra spagnola . . .* Florence F:Pthibault, GB:Lbm, I:Bc, I:Fn	C	M
1640	CARBONCHI, Antonio, *Sonate di chitarra spagnuola en intavolatura francese* Florence E:Mn, I:Fn (2 copies)	B	F
1640	DOIZI DE VELASCO, Nicolao, *Nuevo Modo de . . . la Guitarra . . .* Naples E:Mn	A	Treatise
1640	FOSCARINI, Giovanni Paolo, *Li 5 libri della chitarra alla spagnuola . . .* Rome I:Vnm	B	M
1640	FOSCARINI, Giovanni Paolo, *Inventione di toccate sopra la chitarra spagnuola . . .* Rome (=1640) I:TI	B	M
1643	CARBONCHI, Antonio, *Le dodici chitarre spostate. Libro 2 . . .* Florence D–brd:W, I:Fc, I:Fn, I:Rsc	B	O
1643	CORBETTA, Francesco, *Varii capricci per la ghitarra spagnuola* GB:Lbm	B	M
c.1643	CORBETTA, Francesco, *Varii capricci per la ghitarra spagnuola . . .* Milan (=1643) I:Bc	B	M
1644	MILLIONI AND MONTE, *Vero e facil modo . . . Chitarra spagnola . . .* Venice, F. Vieceri (=c.1627) I:Bc, US:BE (incomplete)	A	O
1645	ANONYMOUS, *Conserto Vago . . . per sonare . . .* I:Bc		X, I, with lute and theorbo
[1645]	DOIZI DE VELASCO, Nicolao, *Nuevo modo de . . . la Guitarra* (=1640)	A	Treatise
1646	CALVI, Carlo, *Intavolatura di chitarra e chitarriglia . . .* Bologna GB:Lbm, I:Bc	B	O, I
1646	GRANATA, Giovanni Battista, *Capricci armonici sopra la chitarriglia spagnuola . . .* Bologna F:Pn, GB:Lbm, I:Bc, I:Fn	B	M
1646	VALDAMBRINI, Francesco, *Libro primo d'intavolatura di chitarra a cinque ordini.* Rome source unknown	C	M
1647	MILLIONI AND MONTE, *Vero e facil modo . . . Chitarra spagnola . . .* Rome and Macerata, A. Grisei I:Bc	A	O

c.1647	VALDAMBRINI, Francesco, *Libro secondo d'intavolatura di chitarra*. Rome source unknown	C	M
1648	ANONYMOUS, *Il primo libro d'intavolatura della chitarra spagnola*. Rome I:Rsc	A	O
1648	CORBETTA, Francesco, *Varii scherzi di sonate per la chitarra spagnola . . . libro quarto* F:Pn, GB:Lbm	B	M
1648	MARCHETTI, Tommasso, *Il primo libro d'intavolatura della chitarra spagnola*. Rome, Catalani I:Rsc	A	O
1648	MERSENNE, Marin, *Harmonicorum libri XII . . .* Paris Many copies including: B:Br, GB:Lbm, US:NYp	C	F, treatise
1648	PESORI, Stefano, *Galeria musicale . . . di Chitarriglia . . .* Verona I-Bc,	B	M
c.1648	PESORI, Stefano, *Lo scrigno armonico . . . opera seconda . . .* Mantua GB:Lbm, I:Bc	B	M
1648	VALDAMBRINI, Francesco, *Il primo libro d'intavolatura della chitarra spagnuola con una regola . . .* Rome source unknown	C	M
1649	FOSCARINI, Giovanni Paolo, *Inventione di toccate sopra la chitarra spagnuola . . .* (=1640) I:PLcom	B	M
c.1650	ABBATESSA, Giovanni Battista, *Ghirlanda di varii fiori . . .* Milan B:Br, GB:Lbm, US:R	A	O
1650?	GRANATA, Giovanni Battista, *Nuove suonate di chitarriglia spagnuola piccicate, e battute . . . opera seconda* I:Bc	B	M
1650	PELLEGRINI, Domenico, *Armoniosi concerti sopra la chitarra spagnuola . . .* Bologna I:Bc, I:Tn, F:Pc, US:BE	B	M
c.1650	PESORI, Stefano, *Toccate di chitarriglia . . . Parte terza . . .* Verona I:Vnm	B	M
c.1650	PESORI, Stefano, *I concerti armonici di Chitarriglia . . .* Verona GB:Lbm	B	M
c.1650	PESORI, Stefano, *Ricreationi Armoniche overo toccate di Chitarriglia . . .* I:Bc	B	M (=toccate . . . parte terza . . . c.1650?)

1651	GRANATA, Giovanni Battista, *Nuova scielta di capricci armonici e suonate musicali in vari tuoni opera terza* . . . Bologna I:Bc	B	M
1652	ABBATESSA, Giovanni Battista, *Intessitura di varii fiori* . . . Rome-Lucca I:Bc	A	O
1652	MILLIONI and MONTE, *Vero e facil modo* . . . *Chitarra spagnola* . . . Venice, G. Bortoli (=c.1627) I:Bc	A	O
1652	PLAYFORD, John, *A Booke of New Lessons for the Cithern and Gittern* . . . GB:Ge		X, F
1653	BANFI, Giulio, *Il maestro della chitara* . . . Milan I:Ma		M
c.1655	BARTOLOTTI, Angiolo Michele, *Secondo libro di chitarra* . . . Rome GB:Lbm, I:Nc	B	M
1655	MARINI, Biagio, *Diversi generi di sonate* . . . *libro III* . . . *op. 22* . . . Venice GB:Ob, I:Bc, PL:WRu (incomplete)		O, acc. to instru- mental music
1659	GRANATA, Giovanni Battista, *Soavi concenti di sonate musicali per chitarra spagnuola, opera quarta* E:Mn, I:Bc, I:VIb, US:Wc	B	M, contains some music for 'chitarra atiorbata'
1659	MILLIONI and MONTE, *Vero e facil modo* . . . *Chitarra spagnola* . . . Venice, G. Batti (=c.1627) CS:Ps	A	O
1660	MARCHETTI, Tomasso, *Il primo libro d'intavolatura della chitarra spagnola* . . . Rome, Francesco Moneta (=1648) F:Pn, I:Bc, I:Vc	A	O
1661	MILLIONI, Pietro, *Nuova corona d'intavolatura di chitarra spagnola novamente ristampata secondo il vero originale di Pietro Millioni* . . . (!) Rome, per l'herede del Mancini (=PICO, 1608) I:Bc	A	O
1663	BOTTAZZARI, Giovanni, *Sonate nuove per la chitarra spagnola* . . . Venice I:Bc	B	M
1663	MARTIN, François, *Pièces de guitairre à battre et à pinser* . . . Paris F:Psg	B	F
c.1665	MARCHETTI, Tomasso (mutilated title page). Rome I:Rsc	A	O
1666	MILLIONI and MONTE, *Vero e facil modo* . . .	A	O

	Chitarra spagnola . . . Venice, C. Bortoli F:Pthibault (=c.1627)		
1666	NIVERS, Guillaume-Gabriel, *Méthode facile pour apprendre à chanter la musique* . . . Paris I:Bc	B	F
1670	CORIANDOLI, Francesco, *Diverse sonate ricercate sopra la chitarra spagnuola* . . . *opera prima.* Bologna I:FEc	B	M
1671	CARRÉ, Sieur de la Grange, Anthoine, *Livre de guitarre contenant plusieurs pièces.* Paris F:Pn	C	F, see 'La Grange' in RISM
1671	CORBETTA, Francesco, *La guitarre royalle dediée au Roy de la Grande Bretagne.* Paris E:Mn, F:Pc, F:Pn, GB:Lbm, GB:Ob, NL:DHgm	B	F
1673	MILLIONI and MONTE, *Vero e facil modo* . . . *Chitarra spagnola* . . . Venice, G. Didini I:Bc, I:Vnm (=c.1627)	A	O
1673	MILLIONI and MONTE, *Vero e facil modo* . . . *Chitarra spagnola* . . . Venice & Macerata, Piccini (=c.1627) D-brd:HVl	A	O
1674	ASIOLI, Francesco, *Primi scherzi di chitarra* . . . Bologna I:MOe	C	M
1674	CORBETTA, Francesco, *La guitarre royale.* Paris F:Pn, I:Bc	B	F
1674	GRANATA, Giovanni Battista, *Novi capricci armonici musicali* . . . *op. quinta.* Bologna D-ddr:Bds, I:Bc	B	M, and trios with violin and gamba
1674	SANZ, Gaspar, *Instruccion de musica sobra la guitarra espanola* . . . (*libro primero*). Saragossa D-brd:Mbs, E:Bc, E:Mn, US:Cn, US:Wc	C	M
c.1675	CARRÉ, Sieur de la Grange, Anthoine, *Livre de pieces de guitarre et musique* source unknown	C	F
1675	SANZ, Gaspar, *Instruccion de musica* . . . (libro primo only). Saragossa (=1674) E:Mn	C	M
1675	SANZ, Gaspar, *Instruccion de musica* . . . (*libros primero & segundo & documentos y advertencias*). Saragossa E:Ayuntamiento de Calanda	C	M
1675	SANZ, Gaspar, *Instruccion de musica* . . . (*libros 1, 2, 3, documentos* Saragossa (3 editions) E:Mn	C	M

1676	ASIOLI, Francesco, *Concerti armonici per la chitarra spagnuola . . . opera terza*. Bologna F:Pc	C	M
1676	MÉDARD, Remy, *Pièces de guitare . . .* Paris Source unknown	B	F
[1676]	MILLIONI, Pietro, *Nuova corona d'intavolatura*		
[1677]	CORBETTA, F.? *Easie Lessons on the Guittar . . . by Seignior Francisco . . .* London (See Pinnell, R., p.254)		
1677	RIBAYAZ, Lucas Ruiz de, *Luz y norte musical . . . la guitarra española . . .* Madrid B:Br, D-brd:B, E:Mmc, E:Mn (3 copies), F:Pc (2 copies), GB:Lbm, US:Cn, US:NYhs, US:SFsc, US:Wc	A	O, I, treatise
1677	RICCI, Giovanni Pietro, *Scuola d'intavolatura . . . la chitarriglia spagnuola . . .* Rome F:Pthibault, GB:Lbm	A	O, also music for mandola
1678	MILLIONI and MONTE, *Vero e facil modo . . . Chitarra spagnola . . .* Venice, G. Zini (=c.1627) GB:Lbm (2 copies), I:Bc, I:MOe, US:Wc	A	O
1680	GRANATA, Giovanni Battista, *Nuovi sovavi concenti . . . et altre . . . a due violini e basso . . . opera sesta.* Bologna I:Bc	B	M
1680	GRÉNERIN, Henri, *Livre de guitare et autres pièces de musique . . .* Paris F:Pc	B	F
c.1680	MATTEIS, Nicola, *Le false consonanse della musica . . . la chitarra sopra la parte . . .* London F:Pthibault	B	F, continuo treatise
1682	MATTEIS, Nicola, *The false consonances of musick . . .* London GB:Ge, GB:Ob (incomplete), I:Bc, US:NYp	B	F, continuo treatise
1682	VISÉE, Robert de, *Livre de guitarre . . .* Paris F:Pn	B	F
1684	GRANATA, Giovanni Battista, *Armoniosi toni . . . op.7.* Bologna GB:Lbm, I:Bc	B	M, and trios for violin and gamba (missing from Lbm copy)
1684	MILLIONI and MONTE, *Vero e facil modo . . . Chitarra spagnola . . .* Venice, G. Zini (=c.1627)	A	O

	I:Bc, US:Wc		
1686	VISÉE, Robert de, *Livre de pièces pour la guittarre* . . . Paris F:Pn	B	F
1688?	DEROSIER, Nicolas, *Douze ouvertures pour la guitare op.5.* The Hague source unknown	B	F
1689	KREMBERG, Jacob, *Musikalische Gemüths-Ergotzung* . . . Dresden A:Wn, GB:Lbm		F, ensemble with several instruments and voice
1690	DEROSIER, Nicolas, *Les Principes de la guitare* . . . Amsterdam B:Br, NL:DHgm	B	F
1692	RONCALLI, Ludovico, *Capricci armonici sopra la chitarra spagnola* . . . Bergamo I:Bc, I:Rsc, I:BGc, GB:Lbm, D-brd:Müs, F:Pthibault, I:Mb, I:Rc	B	M
1694	GUERAU, Francisco, *Poema harmonico, compuesto de varias cifras por el temple de la guitarra espanola* . . . Madrid E:Bc, GB:Lbm, GB:London, R. Spencer's private library	A	I
1696	DEROSIER, Nicolas, *Les principes de la guitare* I:Bc	B	F
1696	NIVERS, Guillaume-Gabriel, *Méthode facile pour apprendre a chanter la musique* . . . Paris B:Br	B	F
1697	SANZ, Gaspar, *Instruccion de musica sobre la guitarra espanola* . . . Saragossa (2 editions) B:Br, CH:Gpu, D-brd:B, E:Mn (2 copies), F:Pc, GB:Lbm, NL:DHgm, US:R	C	M
1698	MICHELE, Antonio di, *La nuova chitarra di regole* . . . Palermo US:Wc	A	O
1699	DEROSIER, Nicolas, *Nouveaux principes pour la guitare* . . . Paris F:Pn	B	F
1705	CAMPION, François, *Nouvelles découvertes sur la guitarre* . . . Paris F:Pc, F:Pn (missing the title page)	B	F
1714	MURCIA, Santiago de, *Resumen de acopañar la parte con la guitarra* . . . Madrid E:Mn, US:Cn, US:LAu	B	M
1730	CAMPION, François, *Addition au traité d'accompagnement* . . . Paris B:Br, F:Pn,	B	Treatise

GB:Ge, NL:DHgm, S:Skma

1737	MILLIONI and MONTE, *Vero e facil modo . . . Chitarra spagnola . . .* Venice, D. Lovisa (=c.1627) F:Pc	A	O
1745	AMAT, Juan Carlos, *Guitarra española . . .* Gerona, Gabriel Bro NL:DHgm	A	O, treatise
c.1750	AMAT, Juan Carlos, *Guitarra española . . .* Gerona, Antonio Oliva E:Bc	A	O, treatise
1752	AMAT, Juan Carlos, *Liçam instrumantal da viola portugueza, ou de Ninfas de cinco ordens . . .* Lisbon E:Mn	A	O, Portuguese edition by Dona Policarpia
c.1752	MINGUET Y YROL, Pablo, *Reglas, y advertencias generales . . .* Madrid E:Bc, E:Bc, E:Mn, F:Pc, GB:Lbm, US:Cn (incomplete), US:NYp (incomplete), US:Wc	A	O, I, treatise
1752	PICA DA ROCHA, João Leite, *Liçam instrumental da viola Portugueza, ou de ninfas, de cinco ordens . . .* Lisbon P:Pm (See Danner, U., p.35)		Amat, 1752?
1758	AMAT, Juan Carlos, *Guitarra española . . .* Valencia, Agustin Laborda E:Mn	A	O, treatise
1758	LAGARDE, De, *Journal de musique (Decembre) . . .* GB:Lbm, GB:London, R. Spencer's private library	A	S
c.1760	ANONYMOUS, *Méthode pour apprendre à jouer la guitarre . . .* Paris US:Wc	A	
c.1761	MERCHI, Joseph Bernard, *Le guide des écoliers de guitarre . . . Oeuvre VIIe . . .* Paris F:Pc (2 copies)	A	S
c.1763	AMAT, Juan Carlos, *Guitarra española y vandola en dos maneras de guitarra . . .* Gerona, Joseph Bro D-brd:B, E:Bim, E:Mn (2 copies), F:Pc, GB:Lbm, GB:London, R. Spencer's private library, I:Mc, US:Cn, US:NH, US:NYcu, US:NYp	A	O, treatise
1763	CORRETTE, Michel, *Les dons d'Apollon. Méthode pour apprendre la guitarre . . . Livre 1ʳ* Paris GB:Lbm	A	F, S
1764	SOTOS, Andrés de, *Arte para aprender . . . la*	A	O, treatise

	guitarra de cinco ordenes . . . Madrid　E:Mn GB:Lbm, US:NYp, US:R, US:Wc		
c.1770	ALBANESE, Egidio Giuseppe Ignazio Antonio, *Les amusements de Melpomène ou IVe recueil d'airs* . . . Paris　F:Pa, F:Pc, GB:London, R. Spencer's private library, US:Cn, US:Wc	A	S
1773	BAILLEUX, Antoine, *Méthode de guitarre par musique et tablature.* Paris　F:Pc	A	F, S
1774	MINGUET Y YROL, Pablo, *Reglas y advertencias para tañer la guitarra* . . . Madrid　E:Mn, GB:London, R. Spencer's private library	A	O, I, guitar part from above c.1752
1777	MERCHI, Joseph Bernard, *Traité des agrémens de la musique exécutés sur la guitarre* . . . *oeuvre XXXVe.* Paris　F:G	A	S
c.1780	AMAT, Juan Carlos, *Guitarra española y vandola, de cinco ordenes y de quatro* . . . Valencia, la viuda de Agustin Laborda　E:Bc, E:Mn, US:R	A	O, treatise
1780	BALLESTERO, Antonio, *Obra para guitarra de seis ordenes* . . .　source unknown	A	Six course
1781	BAILLON, Pierre-Jean, *Nouvelle méthode de guitarre selon le sistème des meilleurs auteurs.* Paris F:Pn	A	S
1786	ALBERTI, Francesco, *Nouvelle méthode de guitarre* . . . Paris　F:Pn	A	S
1788	PORRO, Pierre, *Journal de guitarre* . . . Paris, Porro　F:Pc, US:NYp	A	S
1789	PAIXAõ RIBEIRO, Manuel da, *Nova arte de viola* . . . Coimbra　C:Tu, D-ddr:Bds, E:Mn, F:Pc, GB:Lbm, GB:London, R. Spencer's private library, GB:Ouf, US:AA, US:NH, US:NYp, US:R, US:Wc	A	S, triple courses, treatise
1790	LEMOINE, A. -M., *Nouvelle méthode courte et facile pour la guitarre à l'usage des commençans.* Paris F:Pn	A	S, 5 and 6 string guitar and lyre
c.1790	VIDAL, B., *Nouveaux principes de guitarre* . . . Paris　GB:London, R. Spencer's private library	A	S, I (top line=1st course)
[1792]	MORETTI, Federico, *Principios para tocar la guitarra de seis ordenes* . . . Madrid	A	6 course, treatise

c.1793	PORRO, Pierre, *Six sonates pour la guitare . . . oeuvre XI et 1ᵉʳ livre de sonates . . .* GB:London, R. Spencer's private library	A	S, and violin
c.1795	CHABRAN, Francesco, *Compleat instructions for the Spanish guitar . . .* London GB:Lbm, GB:Ob	A	S
c.1795	GUICHARD, L., *La guitharre rendu facile sans le secours de l'art . . .* Paris F:Pn	A	S
c.1795	VIDAL, B., *Journal de guitare no.1 (& no.10).* Paris GB:London, R. Spencer's private library	A	S
c.1797	GATAYES, *Nouvelle méthode de guitarre . . .* Paris GB:London, R. Spencer's private library	A	S
c.1797	VIDAL, B., *Recueil pour guitarre . . .* Paris GB:London, R. Spencer's private library	A	S
c.1798	GATAYES, Guillaume-Pierre-Antoine, *Nouvelle méthode raisonnée de la guitarre ou lyre . . .* Paris F:BO, F:Pc, GB:London, R. Spencer's private library	A	S
1799	ABREU, Antonio, *Escuela para tocar con perfeccion la guitarra de cinco y seis ordenes . . .* Salamanca E:Bd, GB:London, R. Spencer's private library, US:Wc	A	S, and 6 course, treatise
1799	FERANDIÈRE, Fernando, *Arte de tocar la Guitarra española por música . . .* Madrid A:Wgm, CH:E, E:Mn, GB:London, R. Spencer's private library, US:DN, US:NYp, US:Wc	A	S, 6 course
1799	MORETTI, Federico, *Elementos generales de la musica . . .* Madrid GB:Lbm	A	S, treatise
1799	MORETTI, Federico, *Principios para tocar la guitarra de seis ordenes . . .* Madrid E:Mn, E:Zsc, GB:Lbm, US:NH, US:NYp	A	6 course
1799	RUBIO, Juan Manuel Garcia, *Arte, reglas armónicas para aprehender a templar y puntear la guitarra española de seis ordenes . . .* Madrid E:Mn	A	6 course, treatise
c.1800	AMAT, Juan Carlos, *Guitarra española . . .* Valencia, F. Burguete E:Mn	A	O
c.1800	ANONYMOUS, *Méthode pour jouer de la guitarre . . .* Paris F:Pc	A	S
c.1800	GATAYES, G.-P.-A., *Second méthode de guitare à six*	A	S, 6 single strings

	cordes . . . GB:London, R. Spencer's private library		
c.1800	MORETTI, Federico, *Principi per la chitarra . . .* Naples I:Bc	A	S, 6 course
c.1800	PORRO, Pierre, *Ah! vous dirai-je Maman, varié et modulé pour l'étude de la guitare . . .* Paris GB:London, R. Spencer's private library	A	S
c.1800	PORRO, Pierre, *Les folies d'espagne variées pour l'étude de la guitare.* Paris GB:London, R. Spencer's private library	A	S

2. UNDATED LATE EIGHTEENTH-CENTURY PRINTED SOURCES

AMON, J. A., *Trois sonates pour piano-forte avec guitarre ad libitum*   A:Wgm, D-brd:BNba (pf)

AMON, J. A., *Waltzes, deux eccossaises et une marche pour le piano-forte et guitarre*   A:Wgm

AMON, J. A., *Six waltzes à quatre main pour le piano-forte, avec guitarre obligée* A:Wgm, D-brd:HEms, D-brd:LCH

AMON, J. A., *Divertissement pour la guitarre*   D-brd:F, D-brd:OB

AUBERT, Pierre François Olivier, *Trois duetti pour deux guitarres*   D-brd:Mbs

BOECKLIN, Franz Friedrich Siegmund August von, *Amusement pour le beau monde, sur le violon avec deux guitarres et violoncell*   H:SFm

BRAND, Aloys Carl, *VI Walses pour la guitarre seule . . .* Mainz   D-brd:Mmb

CALEGARI, Francesco, *Rondo per chitarra solo . . . op.3*   D-brd:Mmb

CALEGARI, Francesco, *Tre tema con variazioni per chitarra sola . . . opera 7*   D-brd:Mmb

CALEGARI, Francesco, *La chasse, ouverture de Jean Henri par Méhul, arrangé pour la guitarre seul.* D-brd:Mmb

CALEGARI, Francesco, *Sechs Lectionen für die Guitarre . . . op.11*   D-brd:Mmb

CALEGARI, Francesco, *Six themes avec variations pour la guitarre . . . oeuvre 12*   D-brd:Mmb

CANOBBIO, Carlo, *Six sonates pour la guitarre . . . Oeuvre II.* St. Petersburg   D-ddr:SWl, D-ddr:WRtl

DOISY, Charles, *Grand concerto composé pour la guitare . . .* Paris   CS:Pk (guitar)

DOISY, Charles, *Sonatine pour guitare et violon . . .* Vienna, bureau d'arts et d'industrie CS:N, I:Mc

DOISY, Charles, *Trois duos pour guitare et violons . . .* Amsterdam, A. Kuntze, au magazin de musique   D-brd:B

DOISY, Charles, *Trois duos, extrèmement faciles pour guitare et violons . . . liv. I.* Amsterdam

CS:JIa (guitar)

DOISY, Charles, *Trois duos extrèmement faciles pour guitarre et violons . . . liv. II.* Amsterdam
D-brd:Mbs

DOISY, Charles, *Trois duos concertans et faciles, composés pour guitare et violon.* Paris
S:Skma (guitarre)

DOISY, Charles, *Trois duos concertans composés pour guitare et alto.* Paris   D-brd:Bhm

DOISY, Charles, *Trois duos faciles pour deux guitarres . . . oeuvre 15.* Amsterdam   D-ddr:Dl (b)

DOISY, Charles, *Quatre sonates faciles pour guitare seule.* Paris   CS:Pnm, D-brd:B

DOISY, Charles, *Walses, rondeaux, allemandes, airs variés et faciles . . . composés et arrangés pour une guitare seule . . .* Paris   S:Skma

DOISY, Charles, *Fandango pour une guitarre seule.* Vienna   A:Sca

EPPINGER, Heinrich, *Trio per violino, ghitara, e viola*   A:Wst

GAUDE, F., *24 variations for the flute accompanied by the guitar*   D-brd:Tu

GAUDE, F., *Sechs Walzer und Sechs Eccosaisen für die Guitarre*   D-brd:Tu

GÖPFERT, Carl Andreas, *Op.11. Sonate pour deux guitarres et flûtes . . .* Offenbach, Johann André   CS:Bu, D-brd:OF

GÖPFERT, Carl Andreas, *Op.13 Sonate pour guitare et basson ou alto . . .* Offenbach, Johann André   CS:Bu (kpl.:chitarra, vla, fag)   D-brd:OF

GÖPFERT, Carl Andreas, *Op.15. Sonate für guitarre und flote*   A:Wgm

GÖPFERT, Carl Andreas, *Op.18. Air varié pour guitare et flûte*   D-brd:OF

GÖPFERT, Carl Andreas, *Sonate pour deux guitarres, avec accomp. de flûte*   D-brd:OF

GRAGNANI, Filippo, *Trois duos pour deux guitares, Op.4.* Paris, Richault, Momigny   I:Nc

GRAGNANI, Filippo, *Sestetto per flauto, clarinetto, violino, due chitarre, e violoncello . . . Op.9*
D-ddr:HER

GRAGNANI, Filippo, *Le Déluge . . . Sonate sentimentale pour guitare seule . . . Op.15*   I:Nc

GRAGNANI, Filippo, *Sinfonia per chitarra sola.* Milan, G. Ricordi   CH:Bu

HUBER, J. N., *Trois Fantaisies pour la guitarre seule.* Vienna, Jean Traeg   CS:Pnm

KECK, P. L., *Six pièces pour flûte et guitare.* Copenhagen, C.C. Lose   S:Skma

KRAUS, J., *Sonate pour la guitare . . .* Leipzig, A. Kühnel   D-brd:F

LEMOINE, Antoine Marcel, *Nouvelle méthode de lyre ou guitare à six cordes.* Paris   D-brd:Mmb, F:Pn

L'HOYER, Antoine de, *Grand sonate pour la guitarre . . . Op.12.* Hamburg, Johann August Böhme
S:Skma

L'HOYER, Antoine de, *Six romances pour la guitare . . . Op.XIV.* Hamburg, Johann August Böhme   A:Wn

L'HOYER, Antoine de, *Six romances composées & arrangées pour la guitarre . . . Op.15.* Hamburg, Mees & Co.   S:Skma

L'HOYER, Antoine de, *Air varié pour guitarre.* Offenbach, Johann André   D-brd:OF

L'HOYER, Antoine de, *Air varié pour guitare.* Paris, Pleyel père & fils   D-brd:Mbs

MARTIN Y SOLER, Vicente, *Drei Duetts für zwei Guitarren . . .* Brunswick   D-brd:Mbs

MERCHI, *OP.3. Quatro duetti a due chitarre e sei minuetti a solo . . .* Paris, auteur, Bayard, Le Clerc, et al.   F:Pn, GB:Lbm

MERCHI, *OP.7. Le guide des écoliers de guitarre . . .* Paris   F:Pc (2 ex.)

MERCHI, *OP.20. XVIe Livre de guitarre contenant des airs, romances et vaudevilles . . .* Paris   F:Pc

MERCHI, *OP.22b. Les soirées de Paris . . .* Paris, auteur; Lyon, Castaud   F:Pc

MERCHI, *OP.24. XXe Livre de guitarre . . .* Paris, auteur   F:Pc

MERCHI, *OP.30. XXVIe Livre de guitarre . . .* Paris & Lyon [c.1770]   GB:Lbm

MERCHI, *OP.33. Sei duetti a chitarra e violino con sordina o a due chitarre . . .* Paris, auteur   GB:Ckc

MERCHI, *OP.36. XXXIVe Livre de guitarre . . .* Paris & Lyon   F:Pc
NB. Many of Merchi's other publications are for 'English' guitar.

MIGNARD, *Duo pour la guitarre.* Paris, auteur, Mme Bérault   F:Pn

MOLINO, Valentino, *Grand trio concertant pour violon, alto et guitare . . .* Turin, les frères Reycend & Co.   I:Nc (kpl.:vl, vla, guitarre)

MONZINO, Giacomo, *Divertimenti per chitarra francese . . . op.14a.* Milan, Antonio Monzino I:VEas

MOZART, Wolfgang Amadeus, *Ouverture de l'opéra: Nozze di Figaro, arr. en pour flûte, violon et guitarre, par Gerhard Mayer.* Bonn, N. Simrock   CH:Fk

PHILLIS, Jean Baptiste, *Nouveau recueil de romances, airs, contre-dances, valzes, arrangé pour la lyre ou guitare . . .* Paris, auteur   D-brd:KIl

PHILLIS, Jean Baptiste, *Ah! vous dirai-je Maman. Avec 12 variations pour la guitare.* Paris, Imbault D-brd:Dük

PHILLIS, Jean Baptiste, *Étude nouvelle pour la guitare ou lyre . . .* Paris, Pleyel   DK:Kk

PHILLIS, Jean Baptiste, *Nouvelle méthode pour la lyre ou guitare à six cordes . . .* Paris, Pleyel I:Mc

PICCINI, Nicolo, *Ouverture . . . arrangée pour deux guitares par F. de Fosca.* Bonn-Cologne Simrock   D-ddr:Dl(b)

PLEYEL, Ignace, *Six sonatines per la guitarre . . .* Vienna, Johann Cappi   CS:Pnm

PLEYEL, Ignace, *Quatuor . . . arrangé en duo pour guitare et violon par Oliver Aubert.* Paris, auteur F:Pn

PLEYEL, Ignace, *Polonaise . . . arrangé pour violon et guitarre par François Calegari.* Leipzig, Friedrich Hofmeister   D-brd-Mmb

PLEYEL, Ignace, *Duettino für flöte oder violin und ghitar.* Vienna, Pietro Mechetti   DK:A

PORRO, Pierre-Jean, *Collection de préludes et caprices* . . . Paris, auteur   B:Lc, F:Pn

PORRO, Pierre-Jean, *Nouvelles étrennes de guitarre* . . . Paris, Baillon   F:Pn, US:NYp

RITTER, *Huit sonates pour la guitarre avec un violon* . . . Paris, Sieber; Lyon, Castaud; Dunkirk, Goddaert   CH:Bu

RITTER, Peter, *Notturno pour guitarre, flûte et alto* . . . Mainz, Bernhard Schotts Söhne D-brd:Mmb

ROLLA, Alessandro, *Tre duettini per chitarra e violino.* Zürich, Johann Georg Nägeli   CH:BEk

SCHEIDLER, Christian Gottlieb, *Sonate pour la guitarre* . . . Mainz, Bernhard Schots, Söhne S:Skma

SCHEIDLER, Christian Gottlieb, *Duo pour guitarre et violon* . . . Mainz, Bernhard Schotts Söhne D-brd:B, D-brd:MZsch

SCHEIDLER, Christian Gottlieb, *Duo pour guitarre et violon* . . . Eltville, Georg Zulehner   A:Wn

SCHEIDLER, J. F., *Nouvelle méthode . . . pour apprendre la guitarre ou la lyre* . . . Bonn, N. Simrock CH:Bchristen, D-brd:Tu

SCHLICK, Johann Conrad, *Recueil de petites pièces pour la guitarre* . . . Leipzig, Breitkopf & Härtel D-brd:Lüh, D-ddr:Bds

SCHÖNIGER, *Variations pour deux guitarres.* Bonn, N. Simrock   D-brd:LB

N.B. Further works will be found in succeeding volumes of RISM as they appear.

3. MANUSCRIPT SOURCES

The following list of manuscripts is arranged by location according to country and city. Standard RISM sigla are used (thus, B:Bc= Belgium:Brussels, Conservatoire Royal de Musique). There is still confusion concerning the manuscripts in East Berlin (D-ddr:Bds) due to the lack of recent cataloguing. Following World War II, some manuscripts may have been lost or dispersed to other locations, such as Tübingen.

		TUNING	REMARKS
A (AUSTRIA)			
A:Imf	Mus. MS.533 (early 17th century)		F
A:Imf	no shelf no. (1648) 'Annenberg' Tablature. (See Danner, U.)		I
A:Wn	S.m.9659 (c.1700) 'Ausseer Gitarretabulatur'. (Mod. ed. of selected pieces in Klima A; index in Maier, L.)	A	F, O
A:Wn	Cod.10248 (before 1680) Music by Orazio Clementi. (Index in Maier, L.)	A	F, O

A:Wn	no shelf no. (early 17th century). (4 MS. pages at end of Valderrabano, 1547, containing *differencias de la carabanda, folias, saltarello*; see Ward, V., p.391.)		I (*vihuela*, 6 courses)

B (BELGIUM)

B:Bc	MS.24.135 (early 17th century). (See Turnbull, G., p.40.)		X, I
B:Bc	MS. F.A. VI 8 (early 17th century).	A	O
B:Bc	MS. Littera S, No.5615 (1729) 'Recueil des pièces de guitarre composées par M. François Le Cocq . . . 1729'. (See Pinnell, R., pp.284-7, 306.)	B	F
B:Br	MS. II.5551.D (c.1730-40) IVr Recueil des pièces de Guitarre composées par Mr. François Le Cocq . . . et de differens autres Excellens Maitres: écrites . . . par I.B.L. De Castillion . . .	B	F

CS (CZECHOSLOVAKIA)

CS:Bm	MS.D189 (early 18th century) Contains music by Losy (See Pinnell, R., p.304 and Danner, B., p.50)	B	F
CS: Pdobrovského	MS.b.2 (c.1700)		F, O
CS:Pnm	MS.II.L.a.1 (late 17th century)		F
CS:Pnm	MS.X.L.b.207 (early 18th century)		F
CS:Pnm	MS.X.L.b.208 (early 18th century)		F
CS:Pnm	MS.X.L.b.209 (1639) Contains pieces by Losy and Corbetta (See Pinnell, R., pp.118, 290-1, 306 and Pinnell, A., p.74)	B	F
CS:Pnm	MS.X.L.b.211 (late 17th century) Contains pieces by Losy and Corbetta (See Pinnell, R., pp.291, 306)	B	F
CS:Pu	MS.II.KK75 (early 18th century)		F
CS:Pu	MS.II.KK76a & b (first half of 18th century) (See Danner, B., p.51)		F duets for flute? and guitar
CS:Pu	MS.II.KK77 (late 17th century) 'Pièces composée par le Conte Logis' [c.1645-1721] (See Pinnell, A., p.74)	B	F

D-brd (WEST GERMANY)

D-brd:B	Mus.MS.40085 (c.1640) (For concordances with Carbonchi see Kirkendale, A., p.80; facs. page in Wolf, H., opp. p.186 and Wolf, S., nos. 25 & 37; in 1943, Boetticher, B., p.28, said MS. was in Tübingen (Tu), MS.6.7.61)		M, O
D-brd:B	Mus.MS.40142 (1652) 'Johann Casper von Döremberg' (See Danner, B., p.50)	A	F lost since 1945
D-brd:B	Mus.MS.40160 (mid-17th century) 34 folios; formerly in Dörnberg library (See BE40142, above)		F
D-brd:B	Mus.MS.40163 (c.1660)		O lost since 1945
D-brd:B	Mus.MS.40267 (late 17th century) (See Danner,B., p.50)		F lost since 1945; cithrinchen MS. with a few pieces for mandore (but possibly guitar)
D-brd:B	Mus.MS.40626 (c.1658-1670)		F lost since 1945
D-brd:B	Mus.MS.40631 (late 17th century)		F possibly for mandore
D-brd:DO	Mus.MS.1215 (first half of 18th century) (See Danner, B., p.50)		F
D-brd:KR	H.L81 (c.1650) (Index in Flot.,L.)	B	M 16 pieces at end of lute MS.
D-brd: MZ- federhofer	no shelf no. (late 17th century) Contains pieces by Julien Blovin (See Turnbull, G., p.56; mod. ed. of selection of pieces in *Ausgewählte Stucke aus einer Angelica – und Gitarrentabulatur* . . . Graz, 1967)	B	M, O
D-brd:Mbs	Mus.MS.1522 (c.1660) 'Adelaida di Savoya MS' (See Turnbull, G., p.55)	B	O
D-brd:Rp	MS.[AN] 63 (c.1675) 'Domenico Romani' (See Wolf, H., p.212)	A	O
D-brd:Tu	Mus.MS.40631 (c.1700) (See Danner, U., p.35)		F

DK (DENMARK)

DK:Kk	Ny Kgl. Saml.110 (1736-1744) (14 part-books; the music of N. Diesel; described and indexed in Lyons, D.)	A	F

DK:Kk	GL. Kgl. Saml.377 (1736-1744) (20 part-books; the music of N. Diesel; described and indexed in Lyons, D.)	A	F
DK:Kk	Mus.MS.1879 (1736-45) (See Danner, B., p.50 and Pohlmann, L., p.144.)		

E (SPAIN)

E:Bc	no shelf no. (no. 73 in F. Pedrell, *Catalech de la Biblioteca Musical de la Diputació de Barcelona*, Vol.1, 1908, p.98).		
E:Mn	MS.M.607 (1763) 'Metodo de guitarra'. (See Danner, B., p.50.)		
E:Mn	MS.M.811 (1705) 'Libro de diferentes cifras de gitara, escojidas de los mejer autores'. (See Hudson, I, p.22 and Pinnell, R., p.118.)	B	M
E:Mn	Musica 881 (early 18th century) (MS. copy of thorough bass section of de Murcia's *Resumen de acompanar . . . 1714*.)	B	M
E:Mn	MS.1233 (1763) 'Metodo de guitarra' (translated by 'Joseph Trapero'; see Leon, T., pp.738-9).	B	M
E:Mn	MS.M.2209 (mid 17th century) 'Antonio de Santa Cruz'. (See Pinnell, R., p.306.)		M
E:Mn	MS.5917 'Arte de la Guitarra Autor Joseph Guerrero'. (See Danner, B., p.50.)	A	O (Castilian)
E:Mn	MS.6001 (1593) 'Ramillete de Flores Manuscript'. (Danner, U., p.34 lists this as a guitar tablature of c.1650, but it is definitely for 6-course *vihuela*. (See the modern edition of it by J. J. Rey, Madrid, 1975.)		I (6-course *vihuela*)
E:Mn	MS.14039 (c.1630) 'Francisco Palumbi'. (See Danner, U., p.34.)		O
E: Zaragoza, Biblioteca del Catedral	no shelf no. (c.1700) 'Suma primorosa de la Guitarra, escrito por el Licenciado Manuel Valero, natural de Muniesa, Zaragosa . . .' (See Danner, U., p.35.)	B	M

F (FRANCE)

F:Pm	Rés. 44.108(6) (early 17th century).		X, F
F:Pn	MS.390 (c.1595) 'Palumbi MS.' 'Libro di Villanella/Spagnuol' et Italiane/ et sonate spagnuole . . .' (See Danner, F., pp.6-7 and Devoto, Q., pp.3-16.)	A	O
F:Pn	MS.Rés.Vm⁷374 (early 18th century)		F mostly song accompaniments
F:Pn	MS.Vm⁷675 (c.1665) Contains some Corbetta (See Pinnell, R., p.169)	B	F
F:Pn	MS.Vm⁷6221 (1705-1731) 'François Campion MS.' (See Pinnell, R., p.278 and Hudson, I., p.22)	B	F MS. additions to Campion, 1705
F:Pn	MS.Vm⁷6222 (late 17th century) Pieces by De Visée, etc. (See Strizich, V.)	B	F
F:Pn	MS.Vm⁷6235 (late 17th century)		F mostly song accompaniments
F:Pn	MS.Vm⁷6236 (late 17th century)		F mostly song accompaniments
F:Pn	MS.Vmb ms.58 (c.1660-1665)		F
F:Pn	MS.Vmb ms.59 (c.1690-1710)		F mostly song accompaniments
F:Pn	MS.Rés.Vmc. ms.5 (c.1680)		I, M
F:Pn	MS. F.C.N.Rés.1402 (late 17th century) Pieces by De Visée, etc. (See Pinnell, R., p.265 and Strizich, V.)	B	F
F:Pn	MS. F.C.N.Rés.1956 (c.1750-1760)		F song accompaniments
F:Pn	MS. F.C.N.Rés.F.844 (early 18th century) Pieces by De Visée, etc. (See Pinnell, R., pp.274-77 and Strizich, V.)	B	F
F:Pn	MS. F.C.N.Rés.F.1145 (mid-18th century)		F song accompaniments
F:Psg	MS.2344 'Tablature de Guitarre. 1649' (See Garros, C.)		F also with voice and viols
F:Psg	MS.2349 (mid-17th century) (See Garros, C.)		F also with voice
F:Psg	MS.2351 (mid-17th century) (See Garros, C.)		F also with voice

GB:Cfm	MS.Mus.727 (late 17th century) Joseph Martin y Banez		I
GB:Cmc	MS.2805 (1680) 'A table to the Guitarr shewing the relation of each Frett upon every String . . . by Caesare Morelli . . .'	B	F with solos
GB:En	MS.9452 (mid-17th century) Panmure House no.5		F also lute
GB:HAdol- metsch	MS.II.C.23 (c.1640)		I & O, also lute
GB:Lbm	Stowe 389 (1558) 'Ralph Bowle's MS.'		X, F 1 piece for guitar
GB:Lbm	Add.MS.30513 (c.1570) (Mulliner)		X, F 2 pieces for 'gittern'
GB:Lbm	Add.MS.31440 (late 17th century)		F fragments only in a collection of vocal music
GB:Lbm	Add. MS.31640 (1732) 'Passa-calles y obras de guitarra . . .' 'Santiago Murcia MS.' (See Pinnell, R., pp.241-2)	B	M
GB:Lbm	Add. MS.36877 (early 17th century) 'Villanelle di . . . Giovanni Casalotti'		O song accompaniments
GB: London R. Spencer's private library	no shelf no. (mid-17th century)		X, I
GB: London, R. Spencer's private library	no shelf no. (c.1698)	A	M, O also for lute and mandora
GB: London, R. Spencer's private library	no shelf no. (1733) 'Sonate per il Chitarrone Francese del Sig^r Ludovico Fontanelli 1733' (See Spencer, C. F.)		I 5 courses plus 5 basses, i.e. possibly 'theorboed guitar'
GB:Ob	Mus.Sch.C94 (1660-1684) 'Pieces de Guitarre de diferenda Autheura recueillis par Henry François	B	F

	Gallot'. (See Pinnell, R., pp.266-71, and Gill, G.)		
GB:Ob	Mus.Sch.F.572 (late 17th century)		F a few pieces in a gamba MS.

I (ITALY)

I:Bc	MS.V.280 (c.1614-1617) 'Libros De sonate diverse Alla Chitarra spagnola . . . Sig. Pig. Martinozzini'		I, O
I:Bc	MS. addition to P. Millioni – *Prima scielta de Villanelle*, Rome, 1627		I, O
I:Bu	MS.596 HH2⁴ (late 15th century). (See Dragan Plamenac, Introduction to facsimile edition of Sevilla 5-1-43 and Paris N.A. Fr.4379 (pt.1), New York, 1962, p.6.)		I, 7-course 'viola'
I:Fn	MS.B2521. (See Kirkendale, A., p.52.)	A	O
I:Fn	MS.B2556 (c.1625) 'Questo libro di sonate di chitarra e di Giovanni Antonii'. (See I:FR MS.2793 for same handwriting and some concordances; see Kirkendale, A., p.81 and Pinnell, R., p.45.)	A	O
I:Fn	MS. Landau 175 (c.1635). (See Pinnell, R., p.46; index in Becherini, *Catalogo* . . . 1959, pp.130-1.)		M
I:Fn	MS. Landau 252 (1625?). 'Questo libro di sonate di chitarra spagnuola e di Atto Celli da Pestoia'. (See Pinnell, R., p.45 and Kirkendale, A., p.81.)	A	O
I:Fn	MAGL. XIX 24 (first half of 17th century) 'Arie ad una e due voci col b.c.; sopra il canto le lettere d'intavolatura di chitarra'. (Songs by R. Rontani; see Becherini, *Catalogo* . . . 1959, pp.7-8.)	A	O
I:Fn	MAGL. XIX 25 (first quarter of 17th century). 'Arie e canzoni ad una e due voci con b.c.; in varie composizioni, sopra il canto, le lettere d'intavolatura di chitarra'. (Songs by Brunetti and Caccini; see Becherini, *Catologo* . . . 1959, pp.8-9.)	A	O
I:Fn	MAGL. XIX 28 (mid-17th century). (See Becherini, *Catalogo* . . . 1959, pp.10-11.)		I, possibly 4-course guitar but more likely for mandora

I:Fn	MAGL. XIX 29 (mid-17th century). (See XIX 28.)		I (See above)
I:Fn	MAGL. XIX 143 (c.1625) 'Carbonchi Manuscript' 'Modo insegnato da me Ant.° Carboni [sic] fiorentino per cordor la chitara e poter sonar in compagnia d'altri instrimenti'. (Index in Becherini, *Catologo* . . . 1959, pp.68-9; see Pinnell, R., p.45 and Kirkendale, A., p.81.)	A	O
I:Fr	MS.2774 (c.1620). (See Pinnell, R., p.45 and Kirkendale, A., p.81.)	A	O
I:Fr	MS.2793 (c.1630) 'Canzonette musicali'. (In same hand as MSS.2804 and 2849; see Pinnell, R., p.46, Hudson, I., p.32, Kirkendale, A., p.81.)	A	M and O
I:Fr	MS.2804 (c.1630) 'Q° libro e di Guglielmo Altoviti'. (See MS.2793 above.)	A	M and O
I:Fr	MS.2849 (c.1630). (See MSS.2793 and 2804 above.)	A	M and O
I:Fr	MS.2951 (c.1630). (See Kirkendale, A., p.82 and Pinnell, R., p.46.)	A	M and O
I:Fr	MS.2952 (c.1630). (Music and handwriting as in MS.2951 above; see Kirkendale, A., p.82.)	A	M and O
I:Fr	MS.2973III (c.1630). (See Kirkendale, A., p.82 and Pinnell, R., p.46.)	A	M and O
I:Fr	MS.3121 'Questo libro è di Filippo Baldinotti il quale serve per la sonate della chitarra spagnuola'. (See Kirkendale, A., p.82.)	A	O
I:Fr	MS.3145 (c.1620) 'Questo libro è di Mariotto Tallocci'. (See Pinnell, R., p.45 and Kirkendale, A., p.82.)	A	O
I:MOe	MS.2 (early 17th century). (See Baron, S., p.21)	B	O
I:MOe	MS.3 (early 17th century). (See Baron, S., p.21)	B	O
I:MOe	MS.115 (early 17th century). (See Baron, S., p.21)	B	O
I:MOe	MS. MUS. F1528 (c.1665) 'Autore incerto. Raccolta di balli per la chitarra spagnuola'. (Contains some Corbetta, see Pinnell, R., pp.141, 174.)	B	M
I:MOs	MS. Archivo Ducale Segreto per Materie Musica e Musicisti, Busta Numero IV, e (late 17th century)		O a few pieces amongst music for violin and gamba

I:Nc	MS.1321 (c.1650) 'Canzoni e madrigali, musica diversa . . .' 'Danze Intavolate' f.75-88. (See Pinnell, R., pp.142, 174.)		I
I:Nn	MS.XVII.30 (early 17th century). (See Baron, S., p.24)	B	O
I:Novara Civico Istituto Musicale Brere	no shelf no. (c.1650-1680). (Contains dances and a Toccata). (See Danner, U., p.35.)		
I:PEc	MS.586 (c.1635) 'Sonate per Chitarra'. (Contains engraved portrait of A. Carbonchi; pieces are probably by him; see Kirkendale, A., p.82 and Pinnell, R., p.46.)		M and O
I:PESc	MS.Pc40/7346b (mid-17th century)		O
I:Rsc	MS.A247 (1619) 'Romanus'. (See Kirkendale, A., p.82.)	A	O
I:Rvat	MS. BARB.LAT.4177. (See Danner, B., p.51.)		
I:Rvat	MS. BARB.LAT.4178. (See Danner, B., p.51.)		
I:Rvat	Chigi Codex L.VI.200 (1599) (Dedicated to the Duchessa di Traetta). (See Baron, S., p.24)		
I:Tn	MS. MAURO FOÀ 9 'Intavolatura della Chitarra Spagnola di Desiderio Blas'. (See Kirkendale, A., p.82.)	A	O
I:VEc	MS.1560 (mid-17th century) 'Toccate di Chittariglia . . . Stefano Pesori'		O and M
I:Vnm	IT. IV, 1793 [10649] (c.1657/8). (See Walker, C., p.316.)	A	O
I:Vnm	IT. IV, 1910 [11701] (c.1630). (See Walker, C., p.308n and Pinnell, R., p.46.)	A	M

MEX (MEXICO)

MEX: Mexico City, National Library	MS.15-4-152 (mid-17th century). (See Stevenson, M., p.162)		I probably for mandola
MEX:	MS.1560 (early 18th century). (See	B	M

Mexico City, National Library	Stevenson, M., pp.236-237; Pinnell, R., p.242 and Pinnell, A., p.71.)		
MEX:San Pedro de los Pinos	Coll. of Dr. G. Saldívar; no shelf no. (c.1650) 'Método de Citara' 'Sebastían de Aguirre' (fols. 31-37 contain tablature for 'vihuela de cinco órdenes'; see Stevenson, M., pp.234-235.)	B	M
MEX:San Pedro de los Pinos	Coll. of Dr. G. Saldívar; no shelf no. (mid-18th century) 'Guitar tablature from Guanajuato'. (See Stevenson, M., pp.235-236.)		M

NL (NETHERLANDS)

NL:DHk	MS.133.K.6. (mid-17th century) 'Isabel van Langenhove Manuscript'. (See Boetticher, B., p.36 and Tappert, S., p.78)	B	F
NL:DHgm	MS.4.E.73 (mid-18th century) 'Princes An's Lutebook'. (See Turnbull, G., pp.54-5 and Pinnell, R., p.282; contains 124 pieces including at least 1 by De Visée.)	B	F

P (PORTUGAL)

P:C	MS.97 (mid-17th century) 'Cifras de viola por varios autores, Recolhidas pelo L. Joseph Carneyro Gavares Lamacensa'.	B	M

S (SWEDEN)

S:L	G.34 (late 17th century) 'Daniel Holtz Manuscript' (Lute book with guitar tablature; see Pohlman, L., p.148; Pohlmann also lists G.28 from the same library as a lute book with guitar tablature, but this is incorrect: it is a book of 6-course mandore tablature.)		F probably not guitar but mandore
S:N	MS.FINSP. Nr.9096,2 (late 17th century)		F
S:N	MS.FINSP. Nr.9096,14 (c.1700)		F
S:SK	Mus.468 (1692) 'Guitar book of Hedevig Mörner'		F also music for

			viola da gamba
S:SK	MS.No.493,b. (c.1659-1665) 'Gustav Düben MS.'		F
S:Sk	MS.S.253 (c.1617-1625)		F also music for lute and violin
S: Stockholm Riksarkivet	MS. Ericsbergarkivet Nr.52c (late 17th/early 18th century)		F probably for mandore

US (UNITED STATES)

US: Bloomington, Indiana private library of Prof. Paul Nettle	no shelf no. (late 18th century)		F listed as guitar tablature, but probably for mandore
US:CA	MS.Mus.139 (c.1685) 'Lady Elizabeth Cromwell's guitar book'	B	F
US:NH	no shelf no. (mid-16th century) 'Braye Lute Book' (Property of James M. Osborn)		X, F a few pieces for guitar
US:R	MS.VAULT ML.96.M.435 (late 17th century) MS. copy of Matteis's *Le False Consonanse*	B	F
US:R	MS.VAULT ML.96.L.973 (early 18th century)		F possibly for mandore
US:Wc	M126/C32 (late 17th century) 'Antoine Carré Sieur de la Grange – Livre de pièces de guitarre et de musique dediée à son Altesse Royalle, Madame la Princess d'Orange'. (See Pinnell, R., pp.283, 285)	C	F
US:Wc	MS.M.2.1.18.case. (mid-17th century)		O
US:Wc	MS.M.2.1.T2.17B.case. (mid-17th century)		M

4. MISCELLANEOUS ADDITIONS

	TUNING	REMARKS
Berlin-Grünewald: Wolffheim Library Sign. Nr.62 (late 17th century) (1 folio containing		

'arie (2), marchetta, bergamasca, passamezzo (2)',
listed in Boetticher, B., p.45 as lost).

London: MS. listed in Otto Haas Catalogue 37,
1959, p.24: 'Intavolatura della Spagnuola'
(mid-17th century). (Contains *alfabeto*, texts with
alfabeto.)   O

London: MS. listed in Otto Haas Catalogue 37,
1959, p.24: 'Recueil d'Airs avec accompagnement
de Guitarre' (c.1750). (Contains solos, songs with
accompaniments in French tablature.)

London: Robert Spencer has a large collection
of manuscripts of songs with guitar accompaniments from the late 18th century. Among these
are the following:

   MS. no shelf no. (c.1780) 'Bouleron' 'Trios pour   A   S
la guitarre . . . (guitarre, violon con sordine,
alto)' for 5-course guitar in staff notation;

   MS. no shelf no. (c.1770) French songs and solos.   A   F
Engraved borders on each page; some songs
probably by De la Borde; for 5-course guitar
using French tablature.

Robert Spencer's collection also contains music
for the 5- and 6-course guitar (*chitarra Francese*),
much of it by anonymous composers, but some
by Pietro Pavvini, G. Gazzaniga, Gregorio
Trentin, Giuseppe Milico, Luigi Caruso,
Gabrielle Melia, Antonio Valle, etc.

Boetticher, G., column 198, lists a manuscript
(c.1680) 'chitarra spagnuola', containing
75 pieces by a Sicilian writer, formerly
in the Heyer Collection in Cologne. Its location
is now unknown. In the same paragraph, he lists
three manuscripts formerly at Raudnitz
(Czechoslovakia) in the library of Prince
Lobkowitz (MSS. x h b 207, 209, 211, the last
being a manuscript copy of Matteis's printed
book).

John H. Baron mentions an *alfabeto* MS. of the
early 17th century which was in Parma, but which
he was unable to locate. (Baron, S., p.21.)

Two printed guitar books, now lost, are mentioned in Wessely, I.: Kapsperger's *Intavolatura di chitarra* and his *Intavolatura di chitarra spagnola pizzicata*.

Danner, B. (p.50), lists a 'MUS.MS.acc.4118. c.1645. Alfabeto', as being in D-brd:B, but I have been unable to find any further information about it.

Boetticher, RISM. (pp.41-43) also lists entries for three guitar MSS. offered for sale in the catalogues of the former *Musik-antiquariat* Leo Liepmannssohn:
French tablature entitled: 'Recueil d'airs de guitare' (early 18th century), was listed in *Katalog* 167, 1899 as item nr.1050. Its present whereabouts are unknown.
French tablature (mid-18th century), song accompaniments, listed in *Katalog* 221 as item nr.844. Present whereabouts unknown.
Italian tablature with *alfabeto* (late 17th century), listed in *Katalog* 237 as item nr.963. Present whereabouts unknown.

On p.334, he lists a late 17th-century French tablature belonging to the dealer Hans Schneider in Tutzing (1975).

APPENDIX 2

VOCAL MUSIC ACCOMPANIED BY GUITAR ALFABETO

This list contains the names of the composers of published books, or, where anonymous, the names of the collections. For information as to where these books can be found, look in either BUCM, RISM, or Wolf, H., under the name of the composer, or, where the book is an anonymous collection, look in RISM *Recueils Imprimés XVIe-XVIIe Siècles* under the year of publication.

ABBATESSA, Giovanni Battista	1635
ANON. Giardino Musicale . . .	1621[15]
ANON. Raccolta de varii concerti musicale . . .	1621[16]
ANON. Vezzosetti Fiori . . .	1622[11]
ANON. Canzonette spirituali . . .	1657[1]
ARAGONA, Paolo d'	1616
ARAÑIES, Juan	1624
BERTI, Giovanni Pietro	1624, 1627
BORLASCA, Bernardino	1611
BUSATTI, Cherubino	1644, 1688
CAMARELLA, Giovanni Battista	[c.1633]
CORRADI, Flaminio	1616, 1618
CRIVELLATI, Domenico	1628
FALCONIERI, Andrea	1616, 1619(2)
FASOLO, Giovanni Battista	[1627], 1628
FEDELE, Diacinta	1628
GHIZZOLO, Giovanni	1623
GIACCIO, Orazio	1618
GIAMBERTI, Giuseppe	1623
GRANDI, Alessandro	1626, [1629]
GUAZI, Eleuterio	1622
INDIA, Sigismondo d'	1609, 1621, 1623
KAPSPERGER, Giovanni Girolamo	1610, 1619(2), 1623
KREMBERG, Jacob	1689

LANDI, Stefano	1620, 1637
MANNELLI, Francesco	1636
MANZOLO	1623
MARCHETTI, Tomasso	c.1650
MARINI, Biagio	1622, 1635
MARINONI, Girolamo	1614
MILANUZZI, Carlo	1622, 1623, 1624, 1625, 1628, 1630, 1635
MILLIONI, Pietro	1627(2)
MINISCALCHI	—
MONTESARDO, Girolamo	1612
NIVERS, Guillaume-Gabriel	1666, 1696, 1670, 1702
OBIZZI, Domenico	1627
PERUGINO, Francesco Severi	1626
PESENTI, Martino	1633, 1636
ROMANO, Remigio	1622[20], 1625(4)
RONTANI, Raffaello	1618, 1619, 1620(2), 1622, 1623
SABBATINI, Pietro Paolo	1640, 1641, 1652(2), 165[2]
SEVERI, F.	1626
STEFANI, Giovanni	1618 (destroyed), 1620, 1621, 1622, 1623(2), 1626
TARDITI, Orazio	1628, 1646[9]
VALVASENI, Lazaro	1634
VENERI, Gregario	1621
VINCENTI, Alessandro	1634[7]
VITALI, Filippo	1620, 1622

APPENDIX 3

EIGHTEENTH-CENTURY VOCAL MUSIC ACCOMPANIED BY GUITAR

This list also includes vocal music *arranged* for the guitar. It does not include individual anonymous pieces, but it does include collections of anonymous pieces. Those composers of songs with accompaniments known to be for the 'English' guitar have not been included. All of the following are in staff notation (although a very few include guitar tablature). For information as to where they can be found, look in either BUCM, RISM, or Wolf, H., under the name of the composer, or, where the book is an anonymous collection, look in RISM *Recueils Imprimés XVIIIᵉ Siècle* under the name of the collection.

ABEILLE, J. C. L.

ADRIEN, M. J.

AGUS, G.

AIRS CHOISIS

ALBANESE

ALBERTI, F.

AMBROSCH, J. K.

AMON, J. A.

AMUSEMENT DE SOCIÉTÉ

ARGENS, E. D.

ARIE NOVE DA BATTELO

ASTORGA, G. O.

BARTHELEMON, F. H.

BAUDRON, A. L.

BECZWAROWSKY, A. F.

BEDARD, J. B.

BEFFROY DE REIGNY, L. A.

BENNET

BERCHONI

BERTON, H. M.

BESCHORT, J. F.

BIANCHI, A.

BIANCHI, F. (III)

BLAISE, A.

BLAVET, M.

BOHDANOWICZ, M. von

BOIELDIEU, F. A.

BONESI, B.

BORNHARDT, J. H. C.

BOTHE

BOULERON

BOYÉ

BRUNI, A. B.

CAGÉ

CALEGARI, F.

CAMBINI, G. G.

CANDEILLE, E. J.

CANDEILLE, P. J.

CANNABICH, K. K.

CASTRO

CHABRAN, F.

CHAMPEIN, S.

CHAPELLE, P. D. A.

CHERBOURG, MLLE.

CHERUBINI, L. C. Z. S.

CIFOLELLI, G.

CIMAROSA, D.

COCCHI, G.

COMIEN

CORBAUX

CORRET

CORRI, D.

COULON

DALAYRAC, N. *M.

DAVAUX, J. B.

DAVID, F.

DEDUIT

DELICATI, P.

DELLA MARIA, P. A. *D.

DEMIGNAUX, J. A.

DESARGUS, X.

DESAUGIERS, M. A.

DESHAYES, P. D.

DEVIENNE, F.

DEZÈDE, (N.) A.

DITTERSDORF, K. D.v.

DOBET

DOCHE, J. D.

DOISY, C. (DOIZY-LINTANT, C.)

DU C. . . .

DUCRAY-DUMINIL, F. G.

DUN, A.

DURAND (DUANOWSKI), A. F.

DUVERNOY, F.

ELEY, C. F.

EPPINGER, H.

ÉTRENNES CHANTANTES

ÉTRENNES DE GUITARRE

FOIGNET, C. B.

FONTENELLE, G. DE

FRANZ, J. C.

FRIDZERI (FRIZERI, FRIXER), A. M. A.

FROMANT (FROMENT)

GARAT, P. J.

GAUDRY, R.

GAVEAUX, P.

GENTY, MLLE.

GIROUST, F.

GLOGER, B. von

GLUCK

GODARD

GOSSEC, F. J.

GOUGELET

GOURIET (FILS)

GRESSET, J. –B. –L.

GRÉTRY, A. –E. –M.

GROSHEIM, G. C.

GUICHARD, F.

GUILLAME

GYROWETZ, A.

HASSE, J. A.

HÄUSLER, E.

HEGER, A. D.

HEGGELBACHER, M. A.

HELD, J. T.

HENKEL, A.

HIMMEL, F. H.

HUBER, F.

HURKA, F. F.

HUS, J. B. (FILS)

JADIN, L. E.

JOURNAL D'AIRS [c.1789]

JOURNAL D'AIRS (1796)

JOURNAL DE GUITARRE [1786-87]

JOURNAL DE GUITARRE (1788)

JOURNAL DE GUITARRE

APPENDIX 4
AVAILABLE FACSIMILE EDITIONS OF GUITAR TABLATURES

AMAT, Juan Carlos, *Guitarra española* . . . Lérida (1627)

TECLA (in preparation)

BAILLEUX, Antoine, *Méthode de guittarre* . . . Paris (1773)

MINKOFF

BAILLON, Pierre-Jean, *Nouvelle methode de guitarre* . . . Paris (1781)

MINKOFF

BRIÇEÑO, Luis de, *Metodo* . . . Paris (1626)

MINKOFF

CAMPION, François, *Addition ou traité d'accompagnement* . . . Paris (1730)

MINKOFF

CAMPION, François, *Nouvelles découvertes* . . . Paris (1705)

MINKOFF

CARRÉ, Anthoine, *Livre de guitare* . . . Paris (1671)

MINKOFF

COLONNA, Giovanni Ambrosio, *Intavolatura de chitarra* . . . Milan (1637)

FORNI

CORBETTA, Francesco, *La guitarre royalle* . . . Paris (1671)

MINKOFF

CORBETTA, Francesco, *La guitarre royale* . . . Paris (1674)

FORNI (duet parts missing)

DEROSIER, Nicolas, *Les principes de la guitare* . . . Amsterdam (1690)

FORNI

DOISY, Charles, *Principes généraux de la Guitare* . . . Paris (1801)

MINKOFF

FERANDIÈRE, Fernando, *Arte de tocar la guitara* . . . Madrid (1799)

TECLA

GORLIER, Simon, *Le troysieme livre* . . . Paris (1551)

TECLA (in preparation)

GRANATA, Giovanni Battista, *Novi Capricci Armonici* . . . Bologna (1674)

FORNI

GRÉNERIN, Henri, *Livre de guitare* . . . Paris (1680)

MINKOFF

GUERAU, Francisco, *Poema harmónico* . . . Madrid (1694)

TECLA

LEMOINE, A. M., *Nouvelle méthode* . . . Paris (1790)

MINKOFF

MILLIONI, Pietro and MONTE, Ludovico, *Vero e facil modo* . . .
Rome (1647)

FORNI

MONTESARDO, Girolamo, *Nuova inventione* . . . Florence
(1606)

TECLA (in preparation)

MORETTI, Federico, *Principios* . . . Madrid (1799)

TECLA

MORLAYE, Guillaume, *Le Premiere livre* . . . Paris (1552)
               Le Second Livre . . . Paris (1553)
               Le Quatrieme Livre . . . Paris (1552)

TECLA (in preparation)

RIBAYAZ, Lucas Ruiz de, *Luz y norte musical* . . . Madrid
(1677)

MINKOFF

SANZ, Gaspar, *Instruccion de musica* . . . Saragossa (1674)

IFC

SANZ, Gaspar, *Instruccion de musica* . . . Saragossa (1697)

MINKOFF

SIMON, *Chansons pour la guitarre avec accompagnement de
violon et violoncelle* . . . Paris (c.1760)

TECLA
(songs with guitar accompaniment, violin and cello not listed
in APPENDIX I)

VISÉE, Robert de, *Livre de guitarre* . . . Paris (1682)
          Livre de pieces . . . Paris (1686)

MINKOFF

In addition to these guitar collections there are also available the following items of interest:

MILANO, Francesco da, *Intavolatura de viola overo lauto* . . .
Naples (1536)

MINKOFF

MACE, Thomas, *Musick's Monument* . . . London (1676)

CNRS

MERSENNE, Marin, *Harmonie universelle* . . . Paris (1636)

CNRS

The publishers and addresses are as follows:

FORNI	Arnaldo Forni Editore s.p.a. Via Gramsci 164 40010 Sala Bolognese (Italy)
IFC	Institucion 'Fernando El Catolico' de la Exma Diputacion Provincial (C.S.I.C.) Zaragoza (Spain)
MINKOFF	Minkoff Reprint 46, Chemin de la Mousse 1225 Chene-Bourg/Genève (Switzerland)
TECLA	Tecla Editions Preacher's Court, Charterhouse, London EC1M 6AS (England)
CNRS	Editions du Centre National de la Recherche Scientifique 15, Quai Anatole-France 75700 Paris (France) 'Archivium Musicum' 50125 Firenze Lungarno Guicciardini, 9r. (Planning to publish several Italian guitar books in facsimile.)

BIBLIOGRAPHY

ABBOTT, Djilda and SEGERMAN, Ephraim. 'Strings in the Six-teenth and Seventeenth Centuries' in *Galpin Society Journal*, Vol. XXVII (1974).

Abbott and Segerman S.

'Gut Strings' in *Early Music*, Vol. 4 (1976).

Abbott and Segerman G.

ALLEN, D. Andrew. '*La Guitarre Royalle Dediée au Roy de la Grande Bretagne composee par Francisque Corbett*', 1671. A com-plete transcription, translation, and commentary (dissertation in progress for the University of Manchester)

Allen, G.

APEL, Willi. *The notation of Polyphonic Music 900-1600* (5th ed., Cambridge, Mass., 1953).

ARNOLD, F. T. *The Art of Accompaniment from a Thorough-Bass* (New York, 1965).

BAINES, Anthony. *Musical Instruments through the Ages* (Harmondsworth, 1961).

Baines, M.

European and American Musical Instruments (London, 1966).

Baines, E.

Victoria and Albert Museum Catalogue of Musical Instruments, Vol. II, Non-Keyboard Instruments (London, 1968).

Baines, V.

'Fifteenth-century Instruments in Tinctoris's *De Inventione et Usu Musicae*' in *Galpin Society Journal*, Vol. III (1950).

Baines, F.

BAL, J. 'Fuenllana and the Transcription of Spanish Lute (Vihuela) Music' in *Acta Musicologica*, Vol. XI (1939).

BARON, John H. 'Secular Spanish solo song in non-Spanish sources, 1599-1640' in *Journal of the American Musicological Society*, Vol. xxx, No.1 (1977).

Baron, S.

BELLOW, Alexander. *The Illustrated History of the Guitar* (New York, 1970).

Bellow, I.

BERNER, A., VAN DER MEER, J. H., THIBAULT, G. with the collaboration of Norman Brommelle. *Preservation and Restoration of Musical Instruments* (London, 1967).

BESSARABOFF, Nicholas. *Ancient European Musical Instruments, An Organological Study of the Musical Instruments in the Leslie Lindsey Mason collection at the Museum of Fine Arts, Boston* (New York, 1941).

BINKLEY, Thomas E. 'Le Luth et sa Technique' in *Le Luth et sa Musique* (ed. Jean Jacquot, Paris, 1958).   Binkley, L.

BOBRI, V. *et al.* 'A Gallery of Great Guitars' in *Guitar Review*, Vols. 30 and 32 (August, 1968 and Fall, 1969).

BOETTICHER, Wolfgang. *Studien zur Solistischen Lautenpraxis*   Boetticher, B.
(dissertation, Berlin, 1943).

'Gitarre' in *Die Musik in Geschichte und Gegenwart* (ed.   Boetticher, G.
Friederich Blume, 1949-   ).

Lauten-Und Gitarrentabulaturen des 15. Bis 18. Jahrhunderts,   Boetticher, RISM.
Répertoire international des sources musicales (Kassel, 1979).

BONE, Philip James. *The Guitar and Mandolin* (2nd ed., London, 1954).

BONNER, Stephen. *The Classic Image* (Harlow, 1972).   Bonner, C.

BOYDEN, David D. *Catalogue of the Hill Collection of Instruments in the Ashmolean Museum, Oxford* (Oxford, 1969).   Boyden, C.

BROWN, Howard Mayer. *Instrumental Music Printed Before 1600. A Bibliography* (Cambridge, Mass., 1965).   Brown, I.

Sixteenth Century Instrumentation (Rome, 1973).   Brown, S.

BUCHNER, Alexander. *Musical Instruments: An Illustrated History* (London, 1973).   Buchner, M.

BUETENS, Stanley. 'The Instructions of Alessandro Piccinini' in *Journal of the Lute Society of America*, Vol. II (1969).   Buetens, I.

CARFAGNA, Carlo and CAPRANI, Alberto. *Profilo Storica della Chitarra* (Ancona and Milan, 1966).

CHAPMAN, R. E. (trans.). Marin Mersenne's *Harmonie Universelle (Paris, 1636) The Books of Instruments* (The Hague, 1957).

Chapman, M.

CHARNASSÉ, Hélène. 'A propos d'un récent article sur la méthode pour la guitare de Luis Briçeño' in *Revue de Musicologie*, Vol. LII, No.2 (1966).

Charn, B.

'Sur l'Accord de la Guitare' in *Recherches sur la Musique Française Classique*, Vol. VII (1967).

Charn, A.

CHIESA, Ruggero. 'Storia della letteratura del liuto e della chitarra' in *Il Fronimo*, N.4 (July, 1973).

CHILESOTTI, Oscar. 'Notes sur le guitariste Robert de Visée' in *Sammelbänder der Internationalen Musikgesellschaft*, Vol. IX (1907-8).

CLEMENCIC, René. *Old Musical Instruments* (London, 1968).

COHEN, Albert. 'A Study of Instrumental Ensemble Practice in Seventeenth-Century France' in *Galpin Society Journal*, Vol. XV (1962).

DANNER, Peter. 'Bibliography of Guitar Tablatures 1546-1764' in *Journal of the Lute Society of America*, Vol. V (1972).

Danner, B.

'An Update to the Bibliography of Guitar Tablatures' in *Journal of the Lute Society of America*, Vol. VI (1973).

Danner, U.

'Giovanni Paolo Foscarini and his "Nuova Inventione"' in *Journal of the Lute Society of America*, Vol. VII (1974).

Danner, F.

DELL'ARA, Mario. 'La chitarra nel 1700' in *Il Fronimo*, N.12 (July, 1975).

DENIS, Valentin. *De Muziekinstrumenten in de Nederlanden en in Italië naar hun Afbeelding in de 15e-eeuwsche Kunst* (Louvain, 1944).

DEVOTO, Daniel. 'Que es la Zarabanda?' in *Boletin Interamericano de Musica*, N.51 (January, 1969).

'Poésie et musique dans l'oeuvre des Vihuelistes' in *Annales Musicologiques*, Vol. IV (1956).

DIDEROT, Denis and D'ALEMBERT, Jean le Rond. *Encyclopédie, ou Dictionnaire raisonné des sciences, des arts et des métiers* (Paris, 1751-65).

DOBSON, J. C., *et al*. 'The tunings of the Four Course French Cittern and of the Four Course Guitar in the Sixteenth Century' in *Lute Society Journal*, Vol. XVI (1974).

DONINGTON, Robert. *The Interpretation of Early Music* (New Version, London, 1974).

ESCUDERO, José Castro. 'La Méthode pour la Guitare de Luis Briçeño' in *Revue de Musicologie*, Vol. LI, No. 2 (1965).

EVANS, Tom and Mary. *Guitars: From the Renaissance to Rock* (London, 1977).

FALLOWS, David. '15th-century Tablatures for Plucked Instruments: A Summary, A Revision, and a Suggestion', *The Lute Society Journal*, Vol. XIX (1977).

FEDERHOFER, Hellmut. 'Eine Angelica und Gitarrentabulatur aus der zweiten Halfte des 17. Jahrhunderts' in *Festschrift für Walter Wiora* (Kassel, 1967).

FLOTZINGER, Rudolf. *Die Lautentabulaturen des Stiftes Kremsmunster* (Band II in the series, *Tabulae Musicae Austriacae*, Vienna, 1965).

FORTUNE, Nigel. 'Giustiniani on Instruments' in *Galpin Society Journal*, Vol. V (1952).

FRIZOLI, Patricia. 'The Museo Stradivariano in Cremona' in *Galpin Society Journal*, Vol. XXIV (1971).

GABRY, Gyorgy. *Old Musical Instruments* (Budapest, 1969).

GALPIN, F. W. *Old English Instruments of Music* (4th ed., revised by Thurston Dart, London, 1965).

GARNSEY, Sylvia. 'The Use of Hand-Plucked Instruments in the Continuo Body: Nicola Matteis' in *Music & Letters*, Vol. XLVII (April, 1966).

GARROS, Madeleine and WALLON, Simone. 'Catalogue du fonds musical de la Bibliothèque Sainte-Geneviève de Paris' in *Catalogus Musicus*, Vol. IV (Kassel, 1967).

GEIRINGER, Karl. 'Der Instrumentenname "Quinterne" und die mittelalterlichen Bezeichnungen der Gitarre, Mandola und des Colascione' in *Archiv fur Musikwissenschaft*, Vol. VI (1924).

GILL, Donald. 'The de Gallot guitar books' in *Early Music*, Vol. 6, No.1 (January, 1978).
Gut-Strung Plucked Instruments Contemporary with the Lute (Lute Society Series, London, 1976).

'James Talbot's Manuscript (Christ Church Library Music MS.1187), v. Plucked Strings – The Wire-strung fretted instruments and the Guitar' in *Galpin Society Journal*, Vol. XV (1962).

'Stringing of the Five-Course Baroque Guitar' in *Early Music*, Vol. 3, No. 4 (October, 1975).

GIRAUD, Yves. Note in *Revue de musicologie* (1969).

GRUNFELD, Frederic V. *The Art and Times of the Guitar* (New York and London, 1969).

HALL, Monica J. L. 'Performing music on record 6: the vihuela repertoire' in *Early Music*, Vol. 5, No. 1 (January, 1977).

'The "Guitarra española" of Joan Carles Amat' in *Early Music*, Vol. 6, No. 1 (January, 1978).

Garnsey, U.

Garros, C.

Geiringer, Q.

Gill, G.

Giraud, R.

Grunfeld, A.

Hall, P.

HAMILTON, Mary Neal. *Music in Eighteenth-Century Spain* (Illinois, 1937).

HARRISON, Frank and RIMMER, Joan. *European Musical Instruments* (London, 1964).

HAYES, Gerald. 'Instruments and Instrumental Notation' in *The New Oxford History of Music*, Vol. IV (Oxford, 1968).

HEARTZ, Daniel. 'Parisian Music Publishing under Henry II à propos of four recently discovered guitar books' in *The Musical Quarterly*, Vol. XLVI, No. 4 (1960).   Heartz, P.

'An Elizabethan Tutor for the Guitar' in *Galpin Society Journal*, Vol. XVI (1963).   Heartz, E.

'Les styles instrumentaux dans la musique de la Renaissance, in *La Musique Instrumentale de la Renaissance* (ed. Jean Jacquot, Paris, 1955).

HECK, Thomas Fitzsimmons. 'The role of Italy in the early history of the classic guitar' in *Guitar Review*, No. 34 (1971).

HUDSON, Richard. 'Chordal Aspects of the Italian Dance Style 1500-1650' in *Journal of the Lute Society of America*, Vol. III (1970).   Hudson, C.

'The Music in Italian Tablatures for the Five-Course Spanish Guitar' in *Journal of the Lute Society of America*, Vol. IV (1971).   Hudson, I.

'The Ripresa, the Ritornello, and the Passacaglia' in *Journal of the American Musicological Society*, Vol. XXVII (1974).

'The Concept of Mode in Italian Guitar Music during the First Half of the Seventeenth Century' in *Acta Musicologica*, Vol. XLII (1970).

'The *zarabanda* and *zarabanda Francese* in Italian Guitar Music of the Early 17th Century' in *Musica Disciplina*, Vol. XXIV (1970).

'The *Folia* Dance and the *Folia* Formula in 17th Century Guitar Music' in *Musica Disciplina*, Vol. XXV (1971).

'Further Remarks on the Passacaglia and Ciaconna' in *Journal of the American Musicological Society*, Vol. XXIII, No. 2 (1970).

JACOBS, Charles. *El Maestro* (University Park and London, 1971).   Jacobs, M.

JACQUOT, Jean (ed.). *La Musique Instrumentale de la Renaissance* (Paris, 1955).

Le Luth et sa Musique (Paris, 1958).

JEANS, Susi and OLDHAM, Guy. 'The Drawings of Musical   Jeans and Oldham, D.
Instruments in MS. Add. 30342 at the British Museum' in
Galpin Society Journal, Vol. XIII (1960).

KASHA, Michael. 'A New Look at the History of the Classic Guitar' in *Guitar Review*, No. 30 (1968).

KEITH, Richard. '"La Guitarre Royale": A Study of the   Keith, G.
Career and Compositions of Francesco Corbetta' in *Recherches
sur la Musique Française Classique*, Vol. VI (1966).

'The Guitar Cult in the Courts of Louis XIV and Charles II' in *Guitar Review*, No. 26 (1962).

KINSKY, Georg. *A History of Music in Pictures* (London, 1930).

KIRKENDALE, Warren. *L'Aria di Fiorenza id est Il Ballo del Gran*   Kirkendale, A.
Duca (Florence, 1972).

KLIMA, Joseph. *Ausgewählte Werke aus der Ausseer Gitarre-*   Klima, L.
tabulatur des 18. Jahrhunderts (Heft 10 in the series, *Musik Alter
Meister*, Graz, 1958).

KOCZIRZ, Adolf. 'Die Gitarrekompositionen in Miguel de Fuenllanas Orphenica Lyra (1554)' in *Archiv für Musikwissenschaft*, Vol. IV (1922).

'Die Fantasien des Melchior de Barberis für die siebensaitige Gitarre (1549)' in *Zeitschrift für Musikwissenschaft*, Vol. IV (1922).

KRUMMEL, D. W. *English Music Printing 1553-1700* (London, 1975).

Krummel, E.

LESURE, François (ed.). Pierre Trichet's *Traité des Instruments de Musique* (Neuilly-sur-Seine, 1957).

Lesure, T.

'La Guitare en France au XVIe. Siècle' in *Musica Disciplina*, Vol. IV (1950).

'La Facture instrumentale à Paris au Seizième Siècle' in *Galpin Society Journal*, Vol. VII (1954) and Vol. X (1957).

LESURE, François and THIBAULT, G. *Biographie des Editions d'Adrien le Roy et Robert Ballard, 1551-1598* (Paris, 1955).

LEON TELLO, Francisco José. *La Teoria Española de la Musica en los Siglos XVII y XVIII* (Madrid, 1974).

Leon, T.

LOCKWOOD, Lewis. 'Pietrobono and the Instrumental Tradition at Ferrara in the Fifteenth Century' in *Rivista Italiana di Musicologia*, Vol. X (1975).

Lock, P.

LÜTGENDORFF, Willibald Leo von. *Die Geigen und Lautenmacher vom Mittalter bis zur Gegenwart* (Frankfurt-am-Main, 1922).

LYONS, David B. 'Nathanael Diesel, Guitar Tutor to a Royal Lady' in *Journal of the Lute Society of America*, Vol. VIII (1975).

Lyons, D.

Lute, Vihuela, Guitar to 1800: A Bibliography. (In preparation as part of the *Detroit Studies in Music Bibliography* series, Detroit, Michigan).

Lyons, L.

MacCLINTOCK, C. (trans.). Vicenzo Giustiniani's *Discorso sopra la Musica* (c.1628) (Rome, 1962).

MacClintock, G.

MAHILLON, Victor Charles. *Catalogue descriptif et analytique du Musée Instrumental du Conservatoire Royale de Musique de Bruxelles* (5 vols., Ghent, 1893-1912).

MAIER, Elisabeth. *Die Lautentabulaturhandschriften der Öster-reichischen Nationalbibliothek, 17. und 18. Jahrhunderts* (Band VIII in the series *Tabulae Musicae Austriacae*, Vienna, 1974).

MANNS, Jerry A. 'Gaspar Sanz's *Instrucción de Música sobre la Guitarra . . . 1674*: Translation, Transcription, Commentary' (unpublished M.A. thesis, Case Western Reserve University, 1974).

MARCUSE, Sibyl. *A Survey of Musical Instruments* (London, 1975).

Musical Instruments: A Comprehensive Dictionary (New York, 1966).

MURPHY, Sylvia. 'Seventeenth-Century Guitar Music: Notes on Rasgueado Performance' in *Galpin Society Journal*, Vol. XXI (1968).

'The Tuning of the Five-course guitar' in *Galpin Society Journal*, Vol. XXIII (1970).

'Consort of Guitars' in *Musicology*, Vol. II (1965-67).

'The Guitar (Part I: The Guitar before 1750)' in *The Australian Journal of Music Education*, Vol. XIII (October 1973) also 'The Guitar (Part II: The Guitar from 1750 to the Present Day)' same journal, Vol. XIV (April 1974).

MYERS, Joan. 'Vihuela Technique' in *Journal of the Lute Society of America*, Vol. I (1968).

NELSON, Martha. 'Canarios' in *Guitar Review*, No. 25 (1961).

NESS, Arthur J. *The Lute Music of Francesco Canova da Milano* (Cambridge, Mass., 1970).

NICKEL, Heinz. *Beitrag zur Entwicklung der Gitarre in Europa* (N.P., 1972).

NORTH, Roger. *Roger North on Music, being a selection from his*

Maier, L.

Marcuse, S.

Murphy, R.

Murphy, T.

Myers, V

Ness, M.

essays written during the years c.1695-1728 (transcribed and edited by John Whitridge Wilson, London, 1959).

OSBORNE, James M. (ed.). *The Autobiography of Thomas Whythorne* (Oxford, 1961).

    Osborne, W.

PINNELL, Richard. 'The Role of Francesco Corbetta (1615-1681) in the History of Music for the Baroque Guitar' (Ph.D. dissertation, University of California, Los Angeles, 1976).

    Pinnell, R.

'Alternate Sources for the Printed Guitar Music of Francesco Corbetta (1615-1681)' in *Journal of the Lute Society of America*, Vol. IX (1976).

    Pinnell, A.

PIRROTTA, Nino. 'Music and Cultural Tendencies in fifteenth century Italy' in *Journal of the American Musicological Society*, Vol. XIX, No. 2 (1966).

    Pirr, M.

POHLMANN, Ernst. *Laute, Theorbe, Chitarrone: die Instrumente, ihre Musik und Literatur von 1500 bis zur Gegenwart* (Bremen, 1968).

    Pohlmann, L.

POPE, Isabel. 'La Vihuela y sa Musica en el Ambiente Humanistíco' in *Nueva Revista de Filologia Hispanica*, Vol. XV (1961).

POPE CONANT, Isabel. 'Vicente Espinel as a Musician' in *Studies in the Renaissance*, Vol. V (1958).

POULTON, DIANA. 'How to Play with Good Style by Thomas Sancta Maria' in *Lute Society Journal*, Vol. XII (1970).

    Poulton, H.

'Graces of Play in Renaissance Lute Music' in *Early Music*, Vol. 3, No.2 (April, 1975).

    Poulton, G.

'Notes on Some Differences between the Lute and the Vihuela and their Music' in *The Consort*, No. 16 (July, 1959).

PRAETORIUS, Michael. *Syntagma Musicum II De Organographia* (Wolffenbuttel, 1619; facsimile edition, Kassel, 1929).

    Praetorius, S.

PRAT, Domingo. *Diccionario biografico, bibliografico, critico, de Guitarras, Guitarristas and Guitarreros* (Buenos Aires, 1934).

PRYNNE, Michael. 'A Surviving Vihuela de Mano' in *Galpin Society Journal*, Vol. XVI (1963).

PUJOL, Emilio. 'Significación de Joan Carlos Amat (1572-1642) en la historia de la guitarra' in *Anuario Musical*, Vol. V (1950).

'La Guitare' in *Encyclopédie de la Musique et Dictionnaire du Conservatoire*, Part II, Vol. III (Paris, 1927).

'Les ressources instrumentales et leur rôle dans la musique pour vihuela et pour guitare au XVIe siècle et au XVIIe' in *La Musique Instrumentale de la Renaissance* (ed. Jean Jacquot, Paris, 1958).

El Dilema del Sonida en la Guitarra (Buenos Aires, 1960).

RAVIZZA, Victor. *Das Instrumentale Ensemble von 1400-1550 in Italien* (Bern and Stuttgart, 1970).

ROBERTS, John D. 'The Guitar in 1626' in *Guitar* (May, 1976).

'The Baroque Guitar' in *Guitar* (July, 1974).

'Approbation of Sanz' in *Guitar* (March, 1977).

'Some Notes on the Music of the Vihuelistas' in *Lute Society Journal*, Vol. VII (1965).

'The Flesh-nail Controversy' in *Guitar* (August, 1972).

RUTH-SOMMER, Hermann. *Alte Musikinstrumente* (Berlin, 1920).

SACCONI, S. F. *I 'Segretti' di Stradivari* (Cremona, 1972).

SACHS, Curt. *The History of Musical Instruments* (London, 1942).

Real-Lexicon de Musikinstrumente (2nd revised and enlarged ed., New York, 1964).

Prynne, S.

Ravizza, E.

Roberts, G.

Sacconi, S.

SALAZAR, Adolfo. 'Música, Instrumentos y Danzas en las Obras de Cervantes' in *Nueva Revista de Filogia Hispanica*, Vol. II (1948).

SAMPAYO RIBEIRO, Mário de. 'As "guitarras de Alcácer" e a "guitarra portuguesa"' in *Achegas para a Historia da Música em Portugal*, Vol. IV (Lisbon, 1936).

SENSIER, Peter. 'A Gap in the Story of the Guitar' in *Guitar* (October, 1975).   Sensier, G.

SHERRINGTON, Unity and OLDHAM, Guy (eds.). *Music Libraries and Instruments* (Hinrichsen's 11th Music Book, London, 1961).

SIMPSON, Claude M. *The British Broadside Ballad and its Music* (New Brunswick, New Jersey, 1966).   Simpson, B.

SIMPSON, Glenda and MASON, Barry. 'The 16th-century Spanish Romance: a survey of the Spanish Ballad as found in the music of the vihuelistas' in *Early Music*, Vol. 5, No. 1 (January, 1977).   Simpson and Mason, S

SMITH, Douglas A. 'Baron and Weiss contra Mattheson: In Defense of the Lute' in *Journal of the American Lute Society*, Vol. VI (1973).   Smith, B.

SOURIS, André. *Oeuvres de Dufaut* (Editions du Centre National de la Recherche Scientifique, Paris, 1965).   Souris, D.

SPENCER, Robert. 'Chitarrone, theorbo and arch-lute' in *Early Music*, Vol. 4, No. 4 (October, 1976).   Spencer, C.

'The Chitarrone Francese' in *Early Music*, Vol. 4, No. 2 (April, 1976).   Spencer, C. F.

STEVENSON, Robert M. *Music in Aztec and Inca Territory* (Berkeley, 1968).   Stevenson, M.

Juan Bermudo (The Hague, 1960).

STRAETON, Edmund van der. *La Musique aux Pays Bas avant le XIXe siècle* (8 vols., Brussels, 1867-1888).

STRIZICH, Robert. 'Ornamentation in Spanish Guitar Music' in *Journal of the Lute Society of America*, Vol. V (1972).

Strizich, O.

'A Spanish Guitar Tutor: Ruiz De Ribayaz's *Luz y Norte Musical* (1677)' in *Journal of the Lute Society of America*, Vol. VII (1974).

Strizich, R.

STRIZICH, Robert (ed.). Robert de Visée's *Oeuvres Completes Pour Guitare* (Paris, 1969).

Strizich, V.

STRUNK, Oliver. *Source Readings in Music History* (London, 1952).

Strunk, S.

SUTTON, Julia. 'The Lute Instructions of Jean-Baptiste Bésard' in *The Musical Quarterly*, Vol. LI (April, 1965).

Sutton, I.

TAPPERT, Wilhelm (ed.). *Sang und Klang aus Alter Zeit* (Berlin, 1906).

Tappert, S.

THIBAULT, G. *et al. Eighteenth Century Musical Instruments: France and Britain* (London, 1973).

Thibault, E.

TONAZZI, Bruno. *Liuto, Vihuela, Chitarra e Strumenti Similari Nelle Loro Intavolature* (Ancona and Milan, 1971).

TREND, J. B. *Luis Milan and the Vihuelistas* (London, 1975).

TURNBULL, Harvey. *The Guitar from the Renaissance to the Present Day* (London, 1974).

Turnbull, G.

TYLER, James. 'The Renaissance Guitar 1500-1650' in *Early Music*, Vol. 3, No. 4 (October, 1975).

Tyler, R. G

'A Checklist of music for the Cittern' in *Early Music*, Vol. 2, No.1 (January, 1974).

Tyler, C.

VACCARO, Jean-Michel. *Oeuvres d'Albert de Rippe* I (Editions du Centre National de la Recherche Scientifique, Paris, 1972).

Vaccaro, A.

WALDBAUER, Ivan. 'The Cittern in the 16th Century and its Music in France and the Low Countries' (Unpublished Ph.D. Thesis, Harvard University, 1964).

Waldbauer, C.

WALKER, Thomas. 'Ciaconna and Passacaglia: Remarks on their Origins and Early History' in *Journal of the American Musicological Society*, Vol. XXI (1968).

Walker, C.

WARD, John M. 'The Vihuela de Mano and its Music 1536–1576' (Unpublished Ph.D. dissertation, New York University, 1953).

Ward, V.

'Le problème des hauteurs dans la musique pour luth et vihuela au XVIe siècle' in *Le Luth et sa Musique* (ed. Jean Jacquot, Paris, 1958).

Ward, P.

'Spanish Musicians in Sixteenth Century England' in *Essays in Musicology in Honour of Dragan Plamenac on his 70th Birthday* (eds. Gustave Reese and Robert J. Snow, Pittsburgh, 1969).

WESSELY, Othmar. 'Der Indice der Firma Franzini in Rom' in *Beiträge zur Musikdokumentation Fr. Grasberger zum 60. Geburtstag* (1975).

Wessely, I.

WESSELY-KROPIK, Helene. *Lelio Colista, ein römischer Meister vor Corelli* (Vienna, 1961).

WOLF, Johannes. *Handbuch der Notationskunde* (Leipzig, 1919; reprint, Hildesheim, 1963).

Wolf, H.

WOODFILL, Walter L. *Musicians in English Society from Elizabeth to Charles I* (Princeton, 1953).

WRIGHT, Laurence. 'The Medieval Gittern and Citole: A Case of Mistaken Identity' in *Galpin Society Journal*, Vol. XXX (May 1977).

Wright, G.

ZAYAS, Rodrigo de (ed.). 'Part I, Complete Works of Gaspar Sanz' in *Guitar Review*, No. 40 (New York, 1976).

Zayas, C.

'Gaspar Sanz' in *The Consort*, No. 31 (1975).

ZUTH, Josef. *Handbuch der Laute und Gitarre* (Vienna, 1926; reprint, Hildesheim, 1972).